Annette Wolter

Parakeets

Everything about Acquisition,
Care, Nutrition, and Diseases

With 22 Color Photographs by Outstanding
Animal Photographers
and 30 Drawings by Fritz W. Köhler

Translated by Arthur Freud and Raul E. Ugarte

CHILDRENS PRESS CHOICE
A Barron's title selected for educational distribution
ISBN 0-516-08681-2

First English language edition published in 1982 by Barron's Educational Series, Inc.
© 1978 by Gräfe and Unzer GmbH, Munich, West Germany
The title of the German edition is *Wellensittiche*.

All inquiries should be addressed to:
Barron's Educational Series, Inc.
113 Crossways Park Drive
Woodbury, New York 11797

Library of Congress Catalog Card No. 81-19124
International Standard Book No. 8120-2423-0

Library of Congress Cataloging in Publication Data

Wolter, Annette.
  Parakeets: everything about acquisition, care, nutrition, and diseases.
  Translation of: Wellensittiche.
  Bibliography: p. 72
  Includes index.
  1. Budgerigars. I. Title.
SF473.B8W6413   636.6'864   81-19124
ISBN 0-8120-2423-0   AACR2

Thanks are due to Dr. Juergen Nicolai, Director of the Institute for Bird Research, Wilhemshaven-Rüstersich, for revision of the manuscript, and to the firm of Effem, Verden/Aller for consultation in regard to parakeet nutrition and for assistance with the illustrations.

Photographs
Bielfeld: page 54
Chaffer: pages 63, 64
Effem: front cover; inside back cover; back cover, lower right; page 53
Reinhard: inside front cover; page 9
Wothe: pages 10, 27, 28

PRINTED IN HONG KONG
67   490   17 16 15 14 13 12 11

Table of Contents

3

Table of Contents

A Word Up Front

This book is a statement of love to the parakeets of the world! It is dedicated to all people who live with parakeets and make an effort to be their good friends and protectors. From childhood on, birds (and, above all, parakeets) have belonged in my life. I like these comical miniparrots, their cheerful nature and their charming way of associating with one another. In the course of time, however, I've had to learn that there is more to the maintenance of parakeets than just a love for them. A constant exchange of information with other bird friends and contacts with bird specialists and veterinarians have revealed the manifold problems of parakeet care. I sent out questionnaires prior to working on this book so that I would be properly prepared to answer the many questions that arise from association with parakeets. From the responses of parakeet owners, it was possible to decide where there was uncertainty and what was especially interesting to them. I wish to heartily thank all those who have assisted me with their answers and suggestions and enabled me to prepare this book of advice on this domestic animal.

The results of my inquiry showed that many parakeet lovers don't always know what to do in case of sickness or how they can protect their bird from the dangers that may threaten him in his "living-room apartment." The majority of the people interviewed were also interested in how the wild counterparts of our parakeets live, what behavioral traits the domesticated parakeet has in common with the Australian feral bird, and what these traits mean.

A few statistics speak for themselves: although the parakeet is our favorite domesticated animal (millions live in European and American households), and we therefore ought to be knowledgeable and skillful in our dealings with it, on the average only one of three purchased parakeets survives the first year; only a small percentage of these animals reach their fifth year—and this in a house pet with a life expectancy of 10–14 years. This frightfully high death rate of parakeets is, among other things, the result of ignorance of their nature and of their living habits.

With this book I'd like to help all parakeet lovers to become good bird keepers. With a little goodwill and sufficient knowledge, there is always a way to enable one's parakeet to have a life fit for a bird.

I wish you a lively, healthy parakeet that perhaps will learn to chatter cheerfully and with which you and your family will have many years of enjoyment.

Annette Wolter

From Australia to Europe

Our Parakeet's Ancestors

"Boring creature," I often used to think when I saw a parakeet in someone's home, sitting stupidly on his perch in his cage. I noted only that the bird nudged a little bell or a mirror with his beak, or he preened himself. At that time I knew nothing about parakeets.

An English scientist, Sir John Gould, also described the green midget parrots in Australia as "boring" animals, which "for hours sit motionless in the branches of high trees and utter no sound, although they are somewhat more cheerful early in the morning and late at night." Nonetheless, Gould enjoyed the little parrots so much that he took a pair of them along to England, possibly the ancestors of the home companions that we love and cherish today. That was in 1840, more than 140 years ago.

In England the exotic birds, there called "budgerigars" or "budgies," attracted much attention and provided much enjoyment, but they also aroused greed in people who wanted to own anything that was rare and was an "in" thing, as well as in those who sensed a good opportunity for business. Thus a long period of suffering began for these little creatures from Australia. They were captured by the hundreds of thousands and sent on the week-long sea voyage to Europe. In addition to England, Holland and Belgium were also great transhipping points for this animal freight, of which only a small part ever reached its destination alive. The birds were trapped in gigantic numbers in order to make the undertaking profitable. Unfortunately, the trappers hadn't taken the time to establish beforehand what minimum conditions the birds needed for survival. Of those that managed to survive the painful rigors of transportation, the majority perished upon arrival, even if by good fortune they had been able to obtain the proper nourishment.

As knowledge increased concerning the necessary food and care of parakeets, it finally became possible for the birds to settle in as house pets. Thus the imported parakeets developed into somewhat more cheerful, if also timid, cage birds. They were the pride of their wealthy owners, who had paid a high price for these expensive imports from the fifth continent.

Figure 1 *His owner's finger is a favorite spot for the tame parakeet.*

The Domesticated Bird

Right from the beginning, bird owners were puzzled by the fact that the parakeet females laid their eggs in their cages but did not start to hatch them even though the male partner was present. Quite by accident

From Australia to Europe

it was discovered in the commercial aviaries that the parakeet females squeezed into coconut shells that were supposed to serve as nests for finches. A few females succeeded in hatching eggs in them. The first successful breedings then took place, and a few years after the first large hatch from imported parents, the parakeet was bred and sold in England, Holland, and France. Meanwhile in Australia the capture and export of parakeets were now prohibited by the government.

The Human Being as a Surrogate Partner

A most important discovery was made by chance when a human individual took the place of the hen for young orphaned birds; the "hand-reared" birds became trusting and dependent for life. They accepted their guardian as one of their own and gave him their trust and affection.

The parakeet, by nature accustomed to living in a flock, has such a yen for companionship, even in captivity, that he would prefer to spend day and night on the shoulder, head, or hand of his human partner. In lieu of the feathers of a bird partner, the parakeet will try to groom the skin and hair of his owner; indeed, he even tries to feed his guardian. From the offspring of the wild Australian parent stock there has evolved a "humanized" bird that prefers the end of a pencil in his owner's hand as a perch rather than any branch, that is more avid for human sustenance than for his own seeds, and that enjoys sharing the midday nap of his

friend by perching on his or her nose. Many tame birds develop an effervescent joy of living, a striking intelligence, and a wealth of ideas. They play with their owners and develop very definite patterns of behavior. Owners are always touched and amazed when this little bundle of charming and droll behavior begins to imitate familiar sounds or even to repeat words.

It is always a surprise to breeders that the smallest of all parrots may learn to speak as well as his big cousins. Many parakeets learn to imitate individual words, short sentences, melodies, whistles, or specific sounds. This phenomenon continues to contribute to the great popularity of the parakeet. Also, these pets are easy to keep, make little mess, and require only small amounts of food and a comparatively small cage. They can be kept at very little cost.

Unfortunately, it is not always quite clear to new parakeet owners what a treasure they are bringing home. Only when one truly works intensively with the bird and enables him to live in keeping with his nature, can his little avian personality unfold. One can speak of personality in a parakeet. Each one develops really definite characteristics, an individual temperament, and marked likes and dislikes.

Although their eggs may appear identical, no parakeet is identical to another in appearance, nor do all of these birds have the ability to mimic speech.

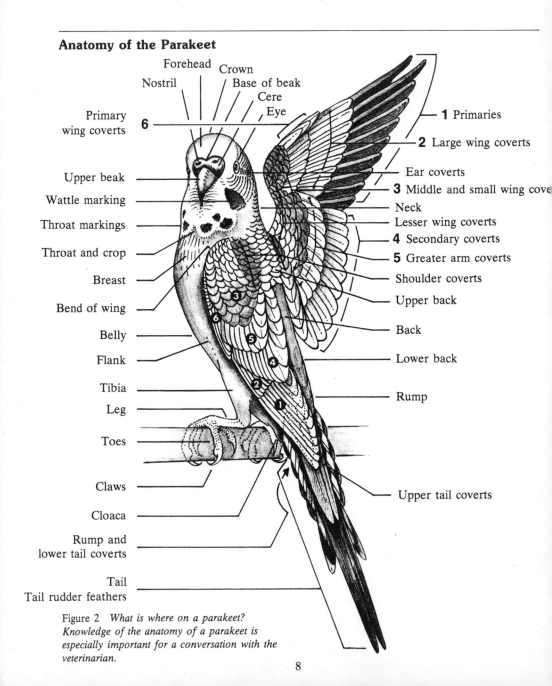

Anatomy of the Parakeet

Forehead

Crown

Nostril

Base of beak

Cere

Eye

Primary wing coverts

6

Upper beak

Wattle marking

Throat markings

Throat and crop

Breast

Bend of wing

Belly

Flank

Tibia

Leg

Toes

Claws

Cloaca

Rump and lower tail coverts

Tail

Tail rudder feathers

1 Primaries

2 Large wing coverts

Ear coverts

3 Middle and small wing cove

Neck

Lesser wing coverts

4 Secondary coverts

5 Greater arm coverts

Shoulder coverts

Upper back

Back

Lower back

Rump

Upper tail coverts

Figure 2 *What is where on a parakeet? Knowledge of the anatomy of a parakeet is especially important for a conversation with the veterinarian.*

8

2 *Feather care is one of the most
rtant and common activities of a parakeet.
r right: the tail feathers are pulled through
eak.*

Information on
the Small Parakeet

The Parakeet and His Relatives

According to the systematic order of zoology, the parakeet belongs in the following category:

Class: Aves (Birds)
Order: Psittaciformes
Family: Melopsittacidae
Genus: *Melopsittacus*
Species: *undulatus*

Flat-tailed parakeets, the closest relatives of the domesticated parakeet, are found in Australia. A few types of these have settled in New Zealand and on the nearby islands. Other parakeets, for example, the wedge-tailed parakeets, live in South America. The domesticated parakeet, however, comes exclusively from the Australian continent. As the smallest flat-tailed parakeet and the commonest bird of Australia, he might be considered the sparrow of the continent.

His name, *Melopsittacus* ("singing parrot"), is explained by his pretty chattering song. The species name, *undulatus,* means "undulating" or "wavy" and refers to the wavy features of the feathers. In England the parakeet is still called a "budgerigar" or "budgerygah." This is the name the little birds brought from their homeland to England. The Australian bushmen called the bird a "betcherrygah." Some sources say that this means "good meal" and serves to remind us that this little fellow was once cooked and eaten.

Size and Appearance

The wild Australian parakeet is somewhat smaller than the domesticated one. His length, which is measured from beak to tail feathers, is from 6½ to 8 inches. He weighs about 1½ ounces. The natural color of the parakeet is grass green. Thus in Holland the bird was at one time known as the "grass parakeet." Strictly speaking, only the lower back, breast, and belly are green. The back of the head, the upper back, and the wings are yellowish with distinct black, wavy lines running crosswise; these patches have a darker appearance than the green. The two long middle feathers of the fan-shaped tail, which forms half of the whole length of the body, are dark blue; the feathers lying inside the fan are green and have a yellow marking. The face of the parakeet is light yellow as far as the throat. At the edge of the mask, as the face is also called, the longish, violet wattle spots grow to the left and right. Growing out of them on each side, toward the interior, are three black throat spots. Each throat spot is about as big as a pinhead.

The black, round pupils of the eyes are surrounded by a white circle of iris. The eyelid closes from bottom to top and is so delicate that in the slumbering bird you can see the pupil shining through. The parakeet beak is an adaptation of the typical parrot beak in proportion to its own size. The sharp, rounded, powerful upper beak reaches over the broad, short, lower beak. It may be light beige, gray-beige, or yellowish. The tongue is dark violet, round, and lumplike and reminds one of a short, fat worm.

Parakeets

Identifying Marks of the Sexes

Both nostrils are located above the upper beak in the smooth cere, which in the adult male is colored a deep blue, and in the female is beige, brownish, or brown. The color of the cere is the most prominent sign of the sex of the bird. The blue color of the cere in the adult male is easy to recognize, even though it can become somewhat paler in weak or sick birds. Only in old age does the male acquire a brownish or cracked cere. The female's cere, on the other hand, is often individually hued; at the beginning of and during hatching, it becomes smooth and light; afterward it once more is darker and easily wrinkled.

The legs and feet of the standard parakeet are powerful and are covered by finely scaled, bluish gray skin. Of the four toes of the foot, the two outer ones are pointed toward the rear and the two inner ones toward the front, as is typical for a climbing bird.

Color Types and Other Standards

Because of their love of colorful birds and, of course, also the ambition to create new breeds, breeders throughout the world have produced parakeets in the most divergent color variations. At shows judges rate the most successful "creation" according to a complicated point system much like the ones used in judging roses or choice wines. The ideal beauty was standardized in England, a land of highly successful animal breeders and geneticists. The standard is perfect and gives an ideal picture of breeding in which body contours, behavior, and feather color and design correspond to well-established expectations. One marvels at these birds in photographs or when viewing them at bird shows, where you can see the most amazing beauties (but rarely a carefree or cheerful parakeet).

There are colors such as light green, olive green, dark green, gray-green, cobalt blue, sky blue, dark blue, violet, mauve, gray, yellow, white, dun green, dun blue, cinnamon green, and cinnamon blue, and combinations such as yellow face, yellow wing, white wing, gray wing, or rainbow colors.

Besides the classification according to color types, parakeets are categorized by still other characteristics, such as "lace wings" or "recessive spots," and birds with these traits are known in the trade as harlequins. There are types with semicircular crests, round crests, and pointed crests. The so-called opals are birds whose wavy characteristics are displayed in a V-shape on the back between the wings. Lutinos are pure yellow birds with black eyes; they also appear with red eyes. Albinos, on the other hand, are pure white birds that often have red eyes but may also appear with black eyes. Strip spots sport two predominant colors distributed bandlike over the breast and belly. Persons interested in breeding parakeets will find references to specialized literature on page 72.

Considerations
before Purchasing

One Bird or a Pair: Whichever Suits Your Life-Style Better

Before you make the trip to a pet store or a breeder, you should weigh carefully whether a single bird or a couple fits better into your living habits. If you are away from home the major part of the day, then a parakeet couple is right for you. A single bird in such a situation will suffer from loneliness. Parakeets are social animals, which in their native Australia travel through the land in flocks and need company—either their own kind or people, who make up for their missing comrades.

Keeping a single bird is proper and defensible if you can devote a lot of time to raising your parakeet and if you'd like it to learn to speak. (The question of male or female would then be of secondary importance.) If you keep only one bird, you should be very much involved with your parakeet—and not merely so that he will learn to talk or whistle. If a parakeet comes into the world in an open aviary among several others of his species and spends his youth there, it will be difficult for the bird to settle down with his new owner. The relationship to the owner will, at best, be one in which the bird loses most of his fear of his human partner and acknowledges him or her as a source of food.

Whoever keeps parakeets in a large aviary can also treat himself to the joy of a manifold companionship of birds. Red cardinals, cockatiels, canaries, long-tailed grass finches, Gouldian finches, lavender finches, pairs of Java rice birds, Cordon Bleus, and zebra finches get along well with parakeets.

How your future parakeet will look is determined when you stand in front of the commercial aviary, in the pet store, or at the breeder. One of the crowd will particularly appeal to you; perhaps because of its color, or because it is especially amusing or lively. Even if the question of male or female is of no particular importance, it still behooves you to know how the sexes are distinguished. I have not found any confirmation up to now of the widespread notion that males are more likely to learn to speak and become friendly much sooner. I know just as many females as males that have at their disposal a considerable vocabulary and have become friendly. In one respect, though, the females distinguish themselves from the males; their tendency to gnaw is fundamentally more pronounced; they constantly search their surroundings for a possible nesting place and to that purpose they test the available material as to its suitability. To be sure, this behavior is modified by time. If the female fails to find a location where she can carve out her niches, then she will give up this type of nesting activity. To protect the cage equipment you can give her branches to gnaw, which you can mount securely in the cage. In other respects there are no clearly defined, essential differences between male and female. Either sex may provide an outspoken, lively bird that after a while will show hardly any fear of human beings—and maybe even a tiny talking genius. It's a gamble. On the other hand, you can also get the opposite from each sex: namely, a frightened bird that out of fear of the unknown willingly stays in its cage, only

Parakeets

timidly attaches itself to a person, and hardly dares to use its voice.

However, I'd like to mention one thing here: the later temperament of a parakeet is largely determined in the weeks from pin feathers to fledgling. If an aviary youth has unpleasant experiences with people, it will develop the full liveliness of its companions only if the guardian is in a position to dispel its mistrust with patience and love. I've learned that this can happen from both of my parakeets.

Charlie and Chrissie—Two Examples of Foster Care

I got Charlie for acquaintances who gave the bird to their elderly father. I selected him from a stock from which my nephew picked a bird for himself the same day. The birds were by no means siblings, but were nursery companions living under the same conditions. My nephew's bird was a harlequin, predominantly white; Charlie was a simple cobalt blue parakeet. My nephew's parakeet was well cared for in his family, was loved by all and received plenty of attention. He was a lively little fellow, at times even aggressive from sheer joy of contact. He didn't speak a word, but he whistled like a street urchin and preferred to imitate the singing of a blackbird.

Charlie, on the other hand, came into the somewhat gloomy apartment kitchen of the elderly father. To be sure, he was promptly provided with food and water, but otherwise lived without any special attention. As a result, he was unable to achieve contact with his owner. When the old gentleman died, nobody in the family wanted to take the bird, so he came to me. During the first few days I hardly dared to approach him; he lay on his stomach, literally trembling from fear. The breeder from whom I asked advice thought that this parakeet could no longer be properly domesticated since he had already lived out the most significant weeks of his life. She offered to take the bird back; she wanted to keep him for breeding purposes. Since I felt sorry for the little bird, I kept him. I made up my mind that he would have an especially good life with me. Despite his youth, which was devoid of friendly contact, Charlie ultimately became a lively, congenial parakeet.

When I had to provide Charlie with a mate, I again went to the breeder. In the large supply of females I discovered a yellow-blue bird in the midst of the tangle of feathers of the many young parakeets that were all crowded together in a protective corner of the carton. She lacked feathers on her upper back and the back of her head; instead there were blood-encrusted places. The breeder explained that this female was a defective bird. When the mother started on her second brood, she drove this little one out of the nest by tearing out her feathers. "She'll never survive, because she still can't eat," the breeder said.

So I took Chrissie with me. For 2 days and 2 nights I fed her at 3-hour intervals; then Charlie took over the task.

Chrissie has been living with us for more than 5 years and has become a

Considerations before Purchasing

self-confident, often even a tyrannical, female.

These little anecdotes indicate how much the guardian of a parakeet can contribute to causing the bird to forget early negative experiences. I would also like to say just this: all other things being equal, try to keep a pair of parakeets.

Male or Female?

If you know that your parakeet is not going to get much attention and will not be able to fly about often, then I advise you to get a pair and to keep the birds in a large cage. The two will accommodate themselves to their circumscribed territory and thus, despite their limited freedom, will develop a charming companionship. It makes no difference whether two males, two females, or one of each sex come together. If two birds of the same sex live in a coupled relationship, one of the two will assume the role of the missing sex partner; therefore one will act as the male, and one as the female. Konrad Lorenz described this very graphically in the example of two female ravens. They copulated with each other—the more powerful of the two in the role of the male, the other as a typical female. Later, when a genuine male was united with them, the hitherto "male" reacted immediately in a typically feminine fashion and finally entered into a genuine union with the new arrival. Of course, one can't transfer this example in detail to parakeets and expect corresponding efforts to bring forth identical results, but the reactions of two parakeets of the same sex will certainly be similar in a community cage.

If, in addition to being a friend to your bird, you are also curious, then bring a suitable mate for your parakeet into the house. In this way you will experience the game of courtship and, finally, the mating from the closest proximity. This drama can be rarely observed in the open air and then only in part. One important point should be added. If you have established a friendship with your single parakeet, if you have accustomed him to living with you and have taught him to speak, these achievements will not vanish because of the presence of a bird partner.

How can you help the parakeet that lives in your home to stay healthy and happy for a long time? I will explain this to you in detail in the following chapters. "Hale and hearty seniors" prove that these birds can live to be 15 or 16 years of age under the proper conditions.

What a Parakeet Needs

It is best that you first buy everything that the bird needs, put his cage in a prearranged place, and only then purchase your new house companion. The poor little fellow is handed to you in a small box, and he's frightened in it. Bring him home in the quickest way and immediately free him from his tiny prison. Things will go most smoothly if his cage, furnished with sand, food, and water, is ready for him.

The Proper Location for the Cage

Birds learn their immediate surroundings very accurately, look upon them as their hunting ground, and are upset if they are separated from them. Consequently, right from the beginning your parakeet requires a secure place in which his cage can remain day and night. This place should be light, should be as quiet as possible, and must afford a good view. Therefore no dark corner should be selected, but also no spot by a window where the full glare of the sun will fall for hours on end, or no place too close to heat. A "traffic crossroad" inside the house, a place that everyone must constantly pass through, is also unsuitable. Above all, the cage must be in a draft-free place protected from the wind, because a parakeet can quickly sicken and die from a draft.

The bird should be able to watch what goes on around him from his cage without standing directly in the midst of the event. Also, locate the cage on the highest point possible, because the bird feels the safest there as he is designed by nature to live in high trees. His instinct tells him that danger (condors) usually threatens from on high; therefore everything that occurs above his head worries him. The immediate vicinity of the television set is also not the right place, because in the evening the bird needs his rest, just like little children.

It's ideal if the cage backs on a wall on one side, as this gives the bird a greater feeling of seclusion. If after deciding on the location you lack a piece of furniture on which the cage can be firmly and safely placed, you should arrange to purchase a stand from which the cage can be hung (Figure 3). These stands are stable and can be easily placed in an ideal spot.

Figure 3 *A cage on a stand can be placed in the most suitable spot in the room with a minimum of effort.*

What a Parakeet Needs

While we're talking about the cage, let me provide two tips from my own experience. First, make the effort and secure an extra sand dish for the cage. This is usually fastened to the bars by two laterally situated metal clamps. The clamps attach around the upper edge of the sand dish and hold this fast with no difficulty. However, just a slight vibration can cause a clamp to slip off and send the sand dish clattering to the floor. Panic in the bird, alarm to you, dirt in the room—all this can be avoided. For every clamp I have provided myself with broad metal hooks, and sometimes I have attached two of them to a wide rubber band. The hooks are latched to the metal clamps on the left and right, and the rubber band presses the sand dish tightly and securely to the bars. The second precautionary measure concerns the stand—more precisely, the supporting pole that is fastened to the weighted base of the stand by means of a heavy-duty screw. In the course of time, just through moving the stand back and forth, the screw can become loosened to a dangerous degree. Therefore check frequently to see whether the screw is on tightly enough.

The birdcage can also be hung on the wall by means of strong pegs and hooks or can be put on a wall shelf.

Suitable Cages

Most people are not in sympathy with the word "cage"; it is reminiscent of imprisonment. Your parakeet, however,

Figure 4 *A large wooden cage with enclosed side walls, roof, and rear wall. Also used as a balcony cage.*

develops a completely different relationship to his cage. For the bird the cage becomes his favorite living quarters—a refuge, a sleeping place, a magic table. However, you should choose a practical cage without unnecessary frills—in short, one that meets the needs of a parakeet (Figures 4–6). First of all let's consider the size. Since on many days the bird will spend more time inside the cage than outside (despite your good intentions about flying time), it is best to select a cage big enough to enable the bird to spread his wings and also to use them if he wants to go from one end of the cage to the other. Such a cage will then be big enough if a partner should later be added. Its dimensions should be at least 40 inches in length, 20 inches in depth, and 32 inches in height. Basically the cage should be rectangular and longer than high. (A smaller cage may be provided just for eating and sleeping.) Its door should stand open during the day as much as possible so that the bird is in it on a voluntary basis.

Parakeets

Depending on the circumstances, however, the bird can remain locked in the smaller cage for many hours.

The lovely older, extended cages of hardwood with metal bars and a secure wooden rear wall are, unfortunately, seldom available any more. They may still

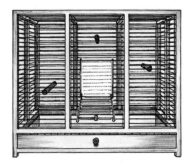

Figure 5 *The ideal room cage for a pair of parakeets. It has straight walls with transverse bars and hardwood frames.*

be found at second-hand markets but are generally in such poor condition that one can have little confidence in their security. Those skilled in home workshop techniques can perhaps build such cages themselves, in any desired size.

With commercially constructed cages you now can choose (according to your taste) between brass and white-painted metal. The appearance makes no difference to the bird, and only size and function are important.

Since we agree on the size, only the question of function remains. The parakeet is a climbing bird. To meet his climbing requirements as fully as possible, the metal bars must run transversely on at least two sides. Having them do so on all four sides

Figure 6 *The frames are metal. The sand trays are removable and therefore easy to clean.*

is even better. The top surface should be flat so that the parakeet can sit on his house. A ladder or other toy should be purchased to provide the bird with diversion and save him from boredom. There should be a smoothly sliding, removable sand tray (Figure 6), at one end of which should be placed dishes for both water and seed. Often a small plastic roof is spread over the dishes to protect the food from dirt. Young parakeets can be so afraid of these roofs that they go hungry in front of full dishes. If this happens, scatter some extra seed on the sand, at least until the bird has grown accustomed to the roofed dishes.

It is extremely important that the door of the birdcage close securely! Parakeets do amazing things with their beaks and are forever looking for activity for them. If the bird has no better object in the cage to occupy him, he will set to work on the door. Many birds have escaped this way. There are miniature swivels with which one can close the door with absolute security.

What a Parakeet Needs

The perches in the cage should be made of hard wood and be thick enough so that the parakeet's foot can just about wrap around them (Figure 7). Birds may develop

Figure 7 *Perches must be thick enough so that the parakeet's foot cannot completely encircle them (left: the proper diameter; right: too thin).*

growths on their toes as a result of perches that are unnaturally smooth or are too thick. To prevent this right from the beginning, get branches from the woods for the cage. They should be about as thick as the store-bought perches (1–1¼ inches in diameter). It is quite all right if some are thicker and others thinner, and if they come from various trees such as oak, elder, poplar, mountain ash, and hazelnut. (If fruit-tree branches are used, make sure that they're free of insecticides! Also, don't use any poisonous branches, such as those from yews.) The branches must be cut properly and fastened securely in place of the perches. A branch that juts out through the bars will definitely be your bird's favorite place outside the cage. Resign yourself to the fact that this was not a one-time task for you. The bird should and will gradually gnaw the branches to bits; then they must be replaced with fresh ones.

A perch that you will be able to replace only with difficulty is the swing. The swing is the favorite place in the cage for many birds and is frequently even the preferred place for sleeping. If there are natural branches in the birdcage, then the bird's toes will have sufficient variety. Once two parakeets live in a cage, the possession of the swing will soon show which is the dominant one of the two. If you are thoughtful, you will provide a second swing, but it must look exactly like the first. Both must be able to swing properly.

Please don't follow the suggestions for impressive home furnishings from magazines, which even advise choosing the color of the bird to match your fabric tapestry or the curtains; and don't under any circumstances buy one of the artful cage monstrosities in pagoda form or country villa style! Even the material from which these models are made—bamboo, reed, or willow—is unsuitable for parakeets. It would be better to build a shelter for your bird yourself.

A Parakeet "Tree" in the House

Without any talent for handicraft you can create a wonderful true-to-life island abode for your bird by means of a "tree" (Figure 8). Depending on the space available, give him a fully grown potted plant; but first make sure that it isn't poisonous, because the parakeet will nibble at it or gnaw it to bits with great enthusiasm. Thus it should

Parakeets

not be an expensive plant. The plant should be placed on a stable platform. Three or four long rods that easily tower over the top of the plant are then vertically inserted into the pot. The rods should be bamboo or tree branches and be fastened by more branches running horizontally and transversely. For this purpose I use tree bark. Even when this cordage is constantly being gnawed away, it holds together until the branches are ready to fall. If you can manage something on a larger scale in the space available, build a barrel out of any kind of material that is in keeping with your furnishings. The barrel can also be

painted if desired. Fill it with dirt, and plant the climbing tree in the dirt. You can also put in an extra-fast-growing climbing tree that will climb up high on the bamboo rods. Thus the entire setup looks pretty and becomes the ideal "tree of life" for the bird or birds. (The barrel has the additional advantage that it catches all the droppings; see Figure 8.)

A Room Aviary

You can erect a room aviary, or have one built, for several parakeet pairs in a bright, draft-free corner if you have lots of living space (Figure 9). This, of course, gives the birds the most generous living area while they are still in your immediate vicinity. This room aviary should be big enough so that one can enter it comfortably to clean it, take care of the birds, and work in it. A double door is provided at a suitable distance so that the birds will not escape when you enter the flight area. Only when the outer door is closed, can the inner door be opened.

The room aviary need not be very wide. Between 3 and 5 feet in depth will suffice; however, it should have a greater length to enable the parakeets, which are skilled flyers, to take at least short flights. If one or two pairs are placed in such a suitable flight area, they will in all likelihood arrive at the mating season and possibly start breeding in a makeshift nest. Hardly any parakeet lover will be able to resist this. Such an owner need only hang the necessary nest boxes in the aviary, and in a

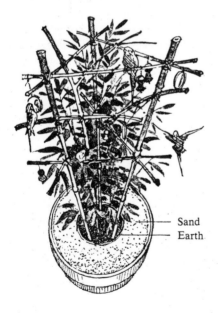

Sand
Earth

Figure 8 *The parakeet tree for the room—very simple to construct and guaranteed to become your bird's favorite spot.*

20

What a Parakeet Needs

Figure 9 *A do-it-yourself room aviary that affords several parakeet pairs extensive space. It is equipped with trees for climbing and sitting, as well as toys and nests.*

few weeks he or she will have not just two pairs but rather a small flock. The next step, an outside aviary, is inevitable for reasons of space. This is the beginning of amateur breeding, and here I must refer you to the pertinent books in which you can find precise technical information on the construction of aviaries. The *Budgerigar Handbook* (see p. 72) has a chapter on building and equipping aviaries.

Food and Water Dishes

Food and water dishes (Figure 10) are part of the normal equipment of a parakeet cage and should be provided with that purpose in mind. Supplementary dishes for food and water may also be provided. Almost any of the types sold in stores may be used, provided that they are not too small. I find semioval or rectangular bowls, for hanging

Figure 10 *There are food bowls of plastic in several colors. They are used for food as well as for water and can be hung in any desired place.*

21

Parakeets

from the vertical bars at the level of the perch, practical and inviting to the birds. Every parakeet gets used to "his own" bowls or to particular food and water dispensers and becomes annoyed at any substitution.

Practical and Useful Supplementary Gadgets

In the course of my wide experience I have found that most of what is provided for the parakeet has proved to be either inferior or impractical. This includes the various pieces of apparatus for supplementary feeding and the inappropriate toys. I would, however, exempt two things from a negative judgment, because they are as practical as they are useful:

- A small metal or plastic bowl for lettuce leaves or other greens.
- A water and a food dispenser (Figure 11).

None of these accessories needs a detailed explanation. I'd merely like to say, regarding the water dispenser, that it is practical because the water inside cannot get dirty. The water dispenser, as well as the food dispenser, proves to be highly advantageous when the bird can't be regularly fed for a day or two, provided that he is accustomed to drinking and to getting his food from such a mechanism. Many birds manage these dispensers on the first try. This is well and good. Many other birds, on the contrary, don't succeed, and there have been cases where parakeets, during their owners' absence, have died of

Figure 11 *The food and water dispensers are filled at the top and yield food or water at the bottom in miniportions. Important: Check daily to see that the mechanism functions properly.*

hunger or thirst in front of full dispensers. In any case you should use the water and food dispensers as supplements to the customary bowls untl the bird has grown accustomed to their use.

The "Bathhouse"

Anyone who maintains that parakeets don't bathe is mistaken. Of course, not all parakeets bathe, but many do so with great relish. Just try it out. A bathtub that hangs in the open cage door (Figure 12) does not cost much. Just make sure at the time of purchase that the "bathhouse" floor is not smooth, but is grooved or provided with a raised platform; otherwise the bird may slip in it and lose interest in bathing temporarily or permanently. If at first your parakeet is

What a Parakeet Needs

afraid of the unfamiliar structure, strew seeds on the floor of the bathhouse and let the bird become comfortable with it. Afterwards fill the bath several times in succession to about 1½ inches high with lukewarm water. If, even after repeated attempts, the bird makes no use of the water, spray him gently with lukewarm water from the faucet. Many parakeets lift and spread their wings happily under a spray and enjoy this kind of bath very much. There are others that will jump into your salad dish in their eagerness to bathe in the wet greens. Should you discover this inclination in your bird, provide such a bath now and then. (Of course, leave out the oil and vinegar and instead have as many water droplets as possible on the greens. These need not necessarily be expensive vegetables and can just as well be dandelions or soft foliage.)

Small plastic bathtubs with a mirror on the floor are also available for parakeet bathing. These bathtubs are probably good for a doll's house but definitely not for a parakeet's. If your bird enjoys a bath, he will want to spread his wings somewhat and let the water reach the undersurface of his wings. Many parakeets prefer to bathe and drink under a gently running faucet. How do the birds discover this possibility, if they don't live right in the kitchen? They probably were so tame that they followed their human companions into the kitchen or bathroom and thus got their first drip bath. You don't have to live with a dripping faucet to accommodate the bird, though; a parakeet accustomed to this bathing style is confident and skillful enough to make clear to you his desire to bathe. For instance, the bird may drink at the dripping faucet and ruffle his feathers excitedly. Be careful with the drip bath, though; the water from the "cold" faucet can sometimes run hot! Always make the finger test first!

Playthings for Diversion

A lone parakeet should always have toys, and even a pair likes to be diverted by them. The female, for example, will work off her energies in front of a mirror, especially if there is no male in close proximity for her to perform for. A little bell for the male, on the other hand, is a wonderful and indispensable item for impressing his female each time they both come into the mating season. He will not only show her by his own characteristic body language what a lively fellow he is but will also ring the bell or rip and tear at the chain. In contrast to some other authors, I

Figure 12 *The bathhouse is hung in the opening of the cage door. A grooved floor is important as the bird can slip on a smooth floor while bathing.*

Parakeets

am in favor of providing toys for parakeets because they simply cannot live true to nature in the home of a human being. They don't have to expand energy or time in search of food, they don't find it necessary to fight off courting rivals for a female, they don't have to be on their guard against enemies and dangers, they seldom or never have parental obligations. We can compensate for the lack of these natural activities by enabling the domesticated parakeet to convert his unused energy and intelligence into play.

So buy your bird playthings, which are available in pet shops. Here are a few suggestions (Figure 13):

Figure 13 *Toys for diversion: bell, ball, roller, tumble-down toy, bird trap. Out of these, the parakeet chooses his surrogate partner and his favorite toy; both are often identical.*

● *A plastic parakeet replica:* One should not frighten young birds with a life-size plastic parakeet: they are also available in "baby sizes" and are then gladly treated as surrogate partners.

● *A little bell:* The most popular are the metallic, shiny bells, which tinkle loudly when the bird strikes the bell with his beak.

● *A mirror* for hanging or as a tumble-down toy.

● *Rings,* which may be used as swings to sit in.

● *Small balls and globes* with plastic parts which resemble the network of lines on a globe. The birds can grip these little balls with their beaks and throw them.

Be careful when buying toys in a store that the strings or chains that secure them are not too long; otherwise the bird could strangle himself with them. As soon as your parakeet is tame, he will certainly seek out small objects in your home to play with. Don't worry about this as long as the components of these objects are not poisonous (such as lead) and that there are no sharp points on which the bird could injure himself.

A Name for the Bird

Give your parakeet a name immediately. It's sensible to call the bird by this name from the first day because he'll then learn that this familiar word applies to him. If you switch between males and females, then think of two names, or one name that suits both sexes. It should be a short name. If the bird has vocal ability (page 34), he will soon repeat his name. According to expert opinion, parakeets find it easiest to repeat words in which an "a," an "i," or a "u" occur. Words with "e" or "o" are apparently less within their grasp. However, even this cannot be generalized—I knew a Peter, a Jocko, and a Morris, all of whom could say their names.

What a Parakeet Needs

Responsibility for the Life of the Bird

For many reasons parakeets are not a suitable gift for Christmas or a birthday. If it's really cold or even damp outside, you should not transport a young bird that up to now has been accustomed only to the cozy nest and the warmth of a shop. Besides, Christmas presents are meant to be brought into the house secretly and concealed until the magic day. How would that be possible with a terrified creature for whom the first hours and days of adjustment are so important? In short, a parakeet as a surprise present can easily be a bad idea. It would be far better for the recipient to decide for himself whether he would like to assume a 15-year responsibility for a bird.

Parakeets are even less suitable as surprise presents for children. Children like to play with their presents in a way that one cannot do with a parakeet that is still timid. Children like to caress an animal and take it in their arms. But this applies only to a robust animal that has the strength to withstand excessive tenderness. Children should have an animal of their own only if their parents are prepared to take responsibility for the care and devotion when the child's interest temporarily or permanently wanes. I know some notable exceptions in which the parakeet was constantly loved and tended by 10- or 14-year-old children. Much more often, however, I have seen the more common behavior where the bird languished slowly, unattended and poorly cared for, in a corner by himself.

Purchase and Settling Down

Plate 3 *The male (blue) puts his female in a ▷ friendly mood. Top left: Attempting to get nearer. Top right: The female reacts aggressively. Bottom left: Making friends by feeding with regurgitated food. Bottom right: The female lets herself be fed.*

There are only three possible ways to come into possession of a healthy young parakeet:

- You may buy the bird in a pet shop.
- You may buy the bird directly from a breeder.
- You may acquire one as a gift because an acquaintance's parakeet pair has had offspring.

If you order your animal from an importer or wholesaler, you must accept what is sent to you and, therefore, can have no role in its selection. The bird arrives at your house after the trauma of transportation. Possible illnesses may not appear until later. You cannot simply just return a sick parakeet or one injured in transit. I am definitely against this kind of animal purchase! If you have no breeder or pet shop in the vicinity of your home, then try in the next larger city or place a small ad in the "Pets Wanted" column of your local newspaper.

What to Look for in a Pet Shop

Look around thoroughly in the pet shop that you have selected. Are the birds kept in sufficiently large cages, rather than in painfully narrow confinement? Do they have fresh seed, some greens, and water? Are the cages clean and strewn with sand? Do the animals get enough light and air? If you notice deficiencies, leave the pet shop and look for another one. There is too great a danger of acquiring a sick bird in the wrong kind of shop. You can be much more confident with a breeder because the success of his or her breeding would be called into question if the birds were not kept under good conditions. Neither a breeder nor a good animal dealer will try to sell you an old bird instead of a young one or will knowingly sell a sick bird.

How to Distinguish between Healthy and Sick Birds

Here are a few points to keep in mind:

- Does the bird of your choice move actively around the cage? Does he eat? Is he occupied with his companions or with an object? If a bird sits silently in a corner with ruffled feathers, he need not be sick, but he may be. Parakeets often sleep during the day; observe a silent bird at least a little longer in order to witness him in action.
- Don't look just at the color of the bird. Also take note of the quality of the feathers. In a young and healthy parakeet they will lie smooth and shiny. The feathers around the cloaca should not be soiled. If they are, this indicates diarrhea and is consequently a sign of an indisposition or even a disease.
- The eyes of a young parakeet should be big and shiny as well as quite round and black (unless the bird is an albino with red eyes).
- Look for clean, straight legs and flawless toes, with claws that are not too long. The scales on the feet should lie smoothly.

Plate 4 *With bars that are close together, the balcony becomes an open flying area. For Charlie the bars provide a welcome opportunity to practice his innate ability to climb.*

- You can recognize the young bird (between 5 and 6 weeks old) by the outstanding "button eyes" and the wavy design or striations that covers the whole little head down to the cere. The throat spots are still small or barely formed. The beak is darker than in a mature parakeet and often somewhat spotted.

- Whether the seller, in keeping with your wishes, succeeds in selecting either a male or a female is mainly a matter of skill. The differences in appearance between young females and males can be established beyond doubt only by experts. One small hint: The female has subtle and delicate light to whitish rings around the nostrils. The cere in young parakeets of either sex is pink, light beige, or light blue.

- Once your choice is made, your bird may be taken out of the cage with a firm but careful grip. While the salesperson holds him, again examine the anal feathers. Also, ask the salesperson to blow the feathers away from this structure so that you can see that the skin around the cloaca isn't red, which could indicate a disease. Stroke the breastbone so that you can establish whether it's convex. A sunken breastbone would again be an indication of sickness.

The Matter of the Band

Before the bird is slipped into the shipping case, he receives a leg band. This band is required by law in the case of imported birds and is an indication that the parakeet was quarantined under government supervison. This means that he will not transmit psittacosis, which in the past was a dreaded disease. This viral disease occurs today in wild birds (especially pigeons) more frequently than in home-bred pets (also see "Diseases," page 44). The band may carry significant information about the bird. If you ask the salesperson to remove the band for you, you may get a "no." But it is worth a try, as it is a fact that parakeets frequently injure the banded leg by getting hung up somewhere and not being able to free themselves. Besides, the banded leg can easily become inflamed and swell up from a band that's too tight. If the bird is banded, therefore, wait until he is tame, and then have the band removed by a veterinarian at your convenience. If you get the band separately from the bird, preserve it carefully as an important document.

Figure 14 *When your parakeet has become tame, you should have his band removed. It is a foreign body for the bird, and he can hurt himself on it.*

Parakeets

The Trip Home

If you can rent a standard, small travel cage, you may spare the animal some of the fright and discomfort that is bound to befall him in a tiny shipping box. The travel cage affords more air, allows more freedom of movement, and also offers protected dark corners into which a frightened young bird may wish to crawl. For example, the parakeets bought in the animal section on the fifth floor of a department store are dropped into a plastic bag and then in the shipping box, and are transported in this manner through the crowded department store and after that are carried elsewhere. Even if a bird escapes being suffocated or squashed, it is still a panicky experience for the little creature.

If you can't rent a travel cage, then, when you buy the bird, at least take a strong traveling box with you. Prepare it beforehand with measurements of about 8 × 16 × 8 inches. Punch many small airholes in the upper side, and make a flap on the narrow side that can open easily. Paste all of the lid edges closed except for the side flap, which remains open. Then, if you receive the parakeet in a small box, carefully open it in the store so that the bird can't get out. You can best prevent this by putting your hand around the opening. Now put the small box into the large one. Close the side flap and secure it additionally by a string. The bird will now get sufficient air and if frightened can slip out of the small box into the larger one. The bird is protected in the best possible way from the wear and tear of trans-portation on the road, in the subway, or on the bus, and thus to some extent he feels secure.

Ground Rules for Settling Down

In the initial weeks you should be cautious in your treatment of the young parakeet and avoid anything that may frighten him:

- Crashes; constant commotion in his presence; above all, slamming of doors.
- Shaking the cage.
- Sudden movements in his presence.
- Grabbing for the bird.
- Glaring light in the evening (only soft light should strike the cage).
- Direct light of television and loud television noises.
- Harsh and dark colors of clothing, frightening hats, roll curlers.
- Disturbance of sleep.

At night always leave the bird in his accustomed place; don't take the cage into another room. If the "bird room" is also the bird's bedroom, all the sounds in there will soon become familiar to the parakeet. If someone sleeps in the same room as the bird, fear of unfamiliar noises at night can drive him to fluttering. In this case it is better to have a 15-watt bulb burning; the bird can orient himself by the night light and will not break out in panic. The light will hardly disturb the sleeper. If the room is occupied almost every night for a long period of time and is therefore illuminated, you must cover the cage with a cloth. Of

Purchase and Settling Down

course, you must then take away the cloth in the morning.

Even if the bird is sleeping in his accustomed surroundings, he can still be panicked in the night by unusual noises such as the loud roar of a car or plane. Then, in a vain attempt to flee, he will storm wildly about in the cage, in which case he can injure himself. If this happens, someone should briefly turn on the light and calm the bird down.

The First Hours and Days at Home

Once you have arrived home, bring the bird in the travel cage to the selected location, or open the carton next to the open cage door and let the bird carefully crawl into his little house. The worst he can do is to slip. The little creature will probably squeeze into the nearest corner of the floor. Let him squat there undisturbed, even if for the time being he doesn't take any of the seed strewn about on the floor of the cage. The parakeet isn't hungry. What is important now is that there be no especially loud noises and that no one come too close to the bird. After a few hours the parakeet will have to stretch his legs. He will turn around a bit, carefully, perhaps to eat the first seeds, perhaps to drink or to timidly clean himself. If during this time nothing frightening happens to the bird, he will soon climb on a perch and shyly survey his new surroundings. Don't get impatient even if it takes 24 hours before the bird gets this far.

If the parakeet on the perch has a secure feeling, he will ruffle his feathers for the first time. Henceforth you can notice this ruffling of the feathers whenever some inner tension in the bird is released, for example, after a fright or after a great strain. Approach the bird often, coming as close as about 3 feet, and speak soothingly. It would be best if a greeting with the bird's name always preceded these approaches. In this initial period move around in the room without rushing. The earlier you tend to your parakeet in the morning, the more happily he will wait for you at the usual hour. In the morning he is especially lively and must eat prodigiously after his night's rest. Arrange it so that the bird still finds food from the day before when he is hungry in the morning and you're still sleeping.

For replenishment of food and water you must place your hand into the cage. Move as carefully as possible and constantly talk soothingly to the bird. The first day, only the bowls need be taken out, emptied, washed out with clear, very hot water, and refilled. The millet spray, which prior to the bird's arrival should have been fastened to the cage with a clothespin, will probably hardly be chewed.

If the parakeet has settled down a little, in the morning, after the replenishment of his seed, he will probably leap greedily onto the freshly filled bowls and behave as if he could not have waited a minute longer for this feeding. During the first days also start offering the bird some parsley, other greens, a piece of apple, or a carrot slice between the crossbars of his little house. If, in the first weeks, the parakeet does not become accustomed to this supplementary nourishment that is so vital to his health, he may be reluctant to try these foods later on.

The First Two Weeks

When the parakeet is no longer timid and nervous, you may try to establish hand contact with him. In the meantime the first millet spray will have definitely been emptied of seed and should be removed. Take fresh millet sprays and pass them into the cage with your hand. If the bird flutters, the attempt was premature and should not be repeated for 2 or 3 days. The next time the bird will probably look covetously at the millet spray from his perch, but will shy away from your hand. Stay perfectly calm and talk to the bird. He will try, with neck outstretched, to reach a few of the tidbits from the greatest possible distance. Remain passive and leave every initiative to the parakeet. If you repeat the game daily at the same time and for the same length of time, the moment will soon come when the parakeet will use your hand as a perch, just like his branches or perches. Be careful, however, of destroying the timidly growing contact when you reach for the bird. A parakeet, whose natural enemy is the condor, has a mortal fear of anything attempting to grasp him. Only really young nestlings let themselves be grasped, because such an embrace may be reminiscent of the womb. Even later you should grasp the bird only in exceptional cases or in emergency situations. After the first successful physical contacts it is time

for the parakeet to have playthings hung in his cage or placed on the floor. Even if the bird only gazes at the toys for several days, he will eventually use them.

Figure 15 *The ball is a favorite plaything of many parakeets. It also often serves as a surrogate partner and is fed and mated with.*

The Third Week

If the parakeet shows no more fear of your hand, you may permit him his first flight in the room. But first close all the doors and windows!

An important consideration before you let your parakeet out of the cage is: Are there curtains in front of the window? The bird doesn't recognize the window pane as such and will regard it as an opening to the outside. He may fly against the pane and quite possibly break his neck. If there are no curtains, before opening the cage, draw the shades down far enough so that only a quarter of the window remains uncovered (if necessary, switch on the electric light for extra illumination). Each day cover less of the window prior to the flying period. This precaution can be completely done away with when the parakeet has recognized the window as a boundary for the room. When you have taken all the necessary precau-

Purchase and Settling Down

tions, open the cage door and leave it to the parakeet as to when he wants to start moving out. Perhaps he will hurry out right away. On the other hand, he may just sit motionlessly and look with astonishment at the opening in his cage, which has just undergone such a big change. Later the bird may venture a second look out the door opening, in which he is now sitting. Perhaps he'll climb out. However things turn out, once the urge to fly overcomes fear, your parakeet will fly through the room for the first time.

Will he succeed in landing on the cage again? Many times this happens right away, but often the bird will land somewhere below because he must recover from the effort of flight, and he will then sit anxiously in the unfamiliar place. Now just give him time. If the parakeet doesn't attempt the return flight alone after about 10 minutes, hold the open cage close to him so that he can enter effortlessly. If you can't reach his new location, let him sit there (if need be, overnight) until he flies back by himself.

If you use cloths or other threatening means to frighten the bird from his place, you will indelibly impress on your parakeet that human beings are his worst enemy.

From now on, you should open the cage door every day at the same hour. The parakeet will not be able to resist the urge to fly and in time will more and more easily find his way back to the cage by himself. When this has happened a few times without difficulty, let the bird out of the cage by offering him your hand. Each time the parakeet is allowed out, extend a finger or the back of your hand to him and lift him out of the cage yourself. The purpose of this is to have the bird become accustomed to your hand and recognize it as an aid.

Once you have become friendly with your parakeet, the moment will come when he will fly to your shoulder for the first time (Figure 16). Walk back and forth in the room with the bird, talk to him, and whistle or sing something to him. He will then sit on your shoulder even longer, because it is a place in which he will feel increasingly secure.

Figure 16 *For the parakeet a shoulder is a good place to "chat" with his owner.*

After the Fourth Week

If you have done everything correctly, by this time your parakeet is tame. You can now play properly with him. A little ball, a little car, a small globe, a tiny bell will interest the parakeet. He will gladly run

Parakeets

after everything that rolls with his beak, particularly items that roll off the table so he can see how they fall.

Pretty soon these "play" hours will be part of your standard daily plan because everybody has such a good time.

Gradually you should also listen to see whether your parakeet babbles to himself. Perhaps you already recognize a few words that you have spoken to him. If so, repeat these over and over as clearly as possible. This is best done by the person most familiar to him. Also keep in mind the fact that your parakeet learns best when there is a minimum of other activity in the room and when he himself is not distracted by any kind of object. If it's quiet and if the bird is not distracted, he will sit on your finger, close to your face, and listen attentively.

You should also try during this tete-a-tete to carefully scratch him. Parakeets that live alone miss the feather grooming that they reciprocally perform while living together with their own species. With the tip of your nose or with your little finger gently stroke against the hairline above the head feathers. If the bird finds this pleasant, he will soon hold out for scratching the parts of his head that he can't reach himself while cleaning. This little "practical tenderness" will deepen the intimacy between bird and owner. The parakeet loves this cosy togetherness as much as he does your voice and the familiar words. Even when he has learned to repeat them effortlessly, he will not want to forgo these "speech lesson hours." If he has the chance, he will often come to you during the day, sit on your finger, lift a leg to his feathers, and look at you expectantly. In this way you may have a natural opportunity to say a new word or a small phrase to him over and over. In England it's supposed to be customary to teach your parakeet your telephone number. If an escapee flies to someone, there is the possibility that the finder will learn the owner's telephone number from the bird and notify him or her. Parakeets not only learn that which one says to them during the "play" and "speak" hours, but also repeat words that they hear often enough, such as phrases used in greeting and departure, swearing, and the "hello" with which we answer the telephone. If you have a bird that is very gifted in talking, you can enlarge his vocabulary by speaking as often as possible to him. The twilight hours are especially good for this because things are quiet, for the most part, and the parakeet does not give his surroundings as much attention as he does during the brighter part of the day. Be assured of this: your parakeet will repeat or imitate most willingly the things that make a great impression on him, those that are often repeated, and above all those that are connected with a special gift from you. The old wives' tale that one must loosen a bird's tongue by slitting it before he can learn to talk is nonsense and—if done—cruelty to an animal. Treats to encourage speech that are offered as special supplementary nourishment may indeed be a tidbit for the parakeet; but his pleasure in speaking will not be aroused and developed through such treats, but solely by the responses of his human owner.

Good Care and Proper Nourishment

A parakeet is easy to take care of, but the little care that he does require must be regularly and thoroughly provided.

- The bowls for drinking water and seed should be rinsed out with hot water, dried thoroughly, and newly filled with seed every day.

- Use a spoon especially adapted for the purpose to remove droppings and seed hulls from the sand. Dirty branches and perches should be either taken out and brushed under hot water or, if nonremovable, brushed several times with fresh, warm water while they are in the cage. (Old toothbrushes are ideally suited for this.)

- The sand should be changed completely twice a week. (If two birds are constantly in the cage, one must change the sand with correspondingly greater frequency.)

- Once a week remove the sand tray from the upper part of the cage and wash it out with hot water.

- Once a month the completely emptied cage should be placed in the bathtub or in a washtub and all sides thoroughly brushed under hot, flowing water and then completely rinsed. Perches or branches and their attachments should be sprinkled with mite spray.

- If the bird has bathed in the "bath-house," it should be rinsed out with hot water, dried, and stored away for the next bath.

- Even the parakeet's toys inside and outside the cage should be washed in hot water once a week, and when necessary even more frequently.

Hot water is the best means for cleaning the cage and all the objects that the bird uses. Washing or cleaning materials (e.g., detergents) are harmful to the parakeet and under some circumstances may even be deadly.

If your parakeet loves his freedom, he may slip out of his cage through the opening while you are cleaning the sand tray. If the doors and windows are closed, this "flight" is not dangerous. Nevertheless, it is advisable to back the cage against the wall or some object in such a way that the opening is blocked.

The sand that is scattered on the cage floor is not only a hygienic measure but also important for the health of the parakeet. The bird takes grit from the sand for daily help in digestion. In addition the sand is enriched with calcium and other minerals. If, instead of sand, you use sanded paper on the cage floor (the type that is sold in stores for this purpose), the parakeet can nibble a few grains of sand from its surface, but he will not obtain valuable minerals at the same time. Here is a compromise suggestion: If you would rather use sanded paper because it raises no dust, then regularly offer the bird a supply of grit in a supplementary bowl.

The Basic Food

Semiripe seeds, the most important food provided for parakeets, are only occasionally found in their Australian environment. During the remaining weeks or months the birds survive with the aid of fully ripe grains of various grasses. The American parakeet receives seeds such as millet, canary, safflower, sunflower, and oats. All these seeds provide him with more or less abundant quantities of carbohydrates, proteins, and fats as well as vitamins and inorganic minerals. The percentages of vitamins and inorganic minerals in these seeds depend on the time of harvest, the storage conditions, and the length of time of storage. One can generally say that properly stored seeds retain their vitamin content up to a year after harvest, and they remain palatable for about 2 years. In seed or pet stores you can buy the proper seed mixture for parakeets loose or in sealed packages produced by firms that manufacture animal food. (These may also be found in supermarkets.) In loose mixtures the quality may be open to doubt. In sealed packages notice the packing date, which is stamped on the bottom of the wrapper or in some other place. If you wish to give your parakeet a seed mixture that provides the required minimum of vitamins you had best buy packages no more than a year old. For years I have provided my parakeets with a seed mixture that pleases me because I know that this balanced combination contains all the necessary minerals and, furthermore, is enriched with iodine seeds. These iodine seeds have proved necessary in maintaining the health of parakeets; they prevent the dreaded goiter. In addition, the packages are provided with the packing date.

In choosing the seed mixture bear in mind two things:

• Whichever seed mixture you may prefer, make the embryo test. Seeds capable of sprouting are likely to contain more valuable nutrients than those that are sterile.

• Each seed mixture provides basic nourishment, but in addition your parakeet needs sprouted seeds, herbs, fruits, and greens.

Sprouted Seeds

As soon as seeds capable of sprouting absorb water, chemical reactions occur in the seeds that induce sprouting. Through this, the vitamins, inorganic minerals, and trace elements that are present are released, and the seeds gain even more value. Soak about half a teaspoon of the regular seed in a little water. The water should cover the seed to a depth of about ¾ inch. Let the seeds stand for 24 hours, and then rinse them thoroughly, using a small strainer. Put them into a flat dish and keep them covered with cellophane for another 24–48 hours. After 24 hours, the sprouted seeds may be served as regular food or as a treat. It is important to note that sprouted seeds deteriorate rapidly. Give this valuable food in the morning in an extra dish. Toward noon, however, remove what the bird has not consumed. This precautionary measure will keep him from eating seed that has already started to decay and thus will prevent illness. With

Good Care and Proper Nourishment

time you will learn precisely the right quantity to supply.

Fruit and Greens

Your parakeet should receive a small portion of fresh greens on a daily basis. These should always be rinsed thoroughly with plenty of lukewarm water and then carefully dried. They should not be stored too long, and wilted greens should never be offered. The greens should include the following: parsley, green spinach leaves, carrot tops, celery leaves, dandelion leaves, and chickweed. If you pick the greens yourself, avoid fields in the vicinity of highways, because poisonous exhaust substances are not completely removed by rinsing and can lead to death.

You may give the bird as much fruit as he likes, provided that the fruit is well washed and dried. It should not be served right from the refrigerator. Rather, it must be at room temperature. Parakeets especially like apple slices, pear slices, and carrot slices. They also enjoy these foods in grated form. Strawberries are considered special tidbits. They prefer to pick off the small seeds that cling to the fruit; however, they also eat the rinds. Parakeets love to nibble on grapes, and they relish sucking the small nodules that remain on the stem after the grapes are picked. The fresh fruits and greens described above are vital for parakeets since the nutrients they provide are either absent from or found in insignificant amounts in seed mixtures. Try to keep offering as great a variety of choices as possible.

Supplementary Vitamins

It is common knowledge that parsley is rich in vitamin A. However, parsley that has been stored too long, is limp, or has been kept by artificial means contains either very little or no vitamin A. This is true of all plants containing vitamins. Vitamins are important to life. The smaller the organism, the more sensitive it is to a diet lacking in vitamins. Thus I advise you that, in spite of the wealth of fresh foods you provide, you enrich the parakeet's drinking water with vitamins. Vitamin preparations from the drugstore may be used, or you can offer products specifically designed for birds, such as Avitron or 8-in-1.

Water or Other Beverages

When I was a beginner, I gave my birds only boiled water. At the University of Munich a veterinarian called my attention to the fact that, while I achieved a certain degree of sterility with boiled water, I also destroyed the nutrients contained in the water, although boiled water or herb tea may be proper in many cases for birds that have fallen sick. After that, only fresh tap water enriched by vitamin preparations was used in my house.

Calcium and Phosphorus

Both minerals are present in only small amounts in the basic food already described. This is compensated for by good

Parakeets

mineral stones for nibbling and for sharpening the beak. These are available in stores. If you keep such a mineral stone constantly available, it may happen that the bird will not touch the stone for weeks and then with a voracious appetite will gnaw it until it crumbles to bits. Keep in mind this advice: "Limestone contains all the material for the building of the skeleton and for the formation of feathers."

Cuttlefish bones are also obtainable in the store. The calcium-rich cuttlefish skeleton is unsuitable for parakeets to nibble on, however, because this salt-containing product can cause egg binding (page 45).

Treats

In addition to the items previously mentioned, the stores offer millet, a precious food that healthy birds should receive daily. In case of sickness it is recommended as the exclusive food.

In the store you can find rings, hearts, or bells to which regular seeds are attached by means of a sugar or honey solution. Since loosening them entails a little nibbling challenge for the birds, they really like these extras.

The Proper Ration of Food

Birds have a high metabolism and consequently require food often during the day. You can observe this yourself. Parakeets do not stay in front of the food bowl for any length of time. They eat, leave, and return frequently, constantly taking just a little seed. One small problem is that the parakeet hulls the seeds skillfully with his beak. The empty shells fall back into the bowl and cover the upper surface. After a few small meals the parakeet is unable to find any seeds under the layer of shells. You must therefore remove the empty shells from time to time. I serve my birds seed in several bowls. Once or twice a day I take out the empty shells with a small teaspoon. Still another dish with seed can be provided outside the cage for birds that are flying outside. The bigger and more shallow the dish, the easier it will be for the birds to locate the full seeds next to the empty shells.

You should also consider the fact that one day you may unexpectedly be prevented from coming home. Food for 2 or 3 days should therefore always be provided. In such a situation even stale drinking water would be better than none.

Don't be concerned if your parakeet attempts to get seed from the cage floor as often as possible. This is a favorite way for him to satisfy his hunger, because he is inclined by nature to hunt for his food on the ground.

Everyday Dangers

Even if your parakeet is tame, healthy, well fed, and high spirited, many types of dangers may threaten him in the home. One must know them in order to be able to prevent them. I will list all the dangers from accidents and injuries that can threaten your parakeet, with the plea that you protect him from them.

Escape

Most birds come to a sad end if they escape and are not lucky enough to find a new home with kind people. There are many opportunities for the parakeet to fly away:

- Doors and windows are left open.
- The bird crawls out of the cage when the sand tray is removed.
- The door of the cage does not shut properly.
- The bars of the cage are loose, and the bird can slip through them.
- Be careful if the bird likes to sit on the head, shoulder, or hat of his owner! In this manner one can unwittingly carry him out of the room and into the open.
- Even visitors can unintentionally take him along until the frightened bird finally flies away.

Many parakeet owners think that, if they have a curtain in front of an open window, the bird cannot fly away. Parakeets, however, like to climb high on the curtain, then slip through a tiny opening above, and climb down again on the other side. By this

Figure 17 *If the bird has not learned to recognize the window pane as a room boundary, he can dash against it and break his neck.*

time they are outside, not from malicious willfulness but because of ignorance.

To prevent this, I had a casement window enclosed with lattice work. A light wooden frame was covered with ½ × ½ inch wire netting and was fastened to the outer window frame.

Even an allegedly absolutely tame parakeet that has always remained in the company of his companion, near an open window, on the terrace, or on the way to take out the garbage or to the automobile, can be panicked by a loud sound and be speedily lost from sight. He may not find his way back, and his fear of the unknown world will increase the chances of his flying away and becoming permanently lost.

Flying away and being lost is the greatest danger to your parakeet. There are others, however, and an overview of dangers follows.

Parakeets

Catalog of Dangers

Source of Danger	Consequences
Drafts from open doors and windows	Parakeets are extremely sensitive to even a brief exposure to drafts: catching cold, sore throat, pneumonia!
Full glare of the sun, over-heated rooms	The bird can't retreat into the shade: heat stroke!
Sudden temperature changes	Room temperatures of between 75°F and 45°F are acceptable. However, the bird must gradually be acclimated to new temperature.
Spaces between the wall and the furniture	Slipping down, getting squeezed!
Bookcases	The bird can crawl behind the books, and will not come out without assistance.
Drawers, closets	The curious bird likes to investigate the contents of open drawers and closets. If he's unnoticed and locked in, he can starve or suffocate.
Kitchen	Fumes and vapors can suffocate him. Necessary ventilation in this generally overheated room can lead to colds. Hot pots or dishes with hot contents: scalding, drowning! Hot stove burners: burning, death by incineration! Residue of detergents: poisoning!
Bathroom	Open window: flying away! Open toilet: slipping inside, drowning! Residue of detergents and chemicals: poisoning!
Window panes, glass panes, glass block walls	Flying against them: brain concussion, skull or neck fracture!
Doors	Getting squeezed, getting crushed!
Containers of water (pails, vases, basins)	Slipping inside, drowning! (The foam on the upper surface of the water is seen as a land surface.)
Filled tubs and washbasins	Drowning!
Ovens, electrical appliances	Burning or death by incineration!
Electric cables, wall sockets	A parakeet that nibbles these can receive a severe shock.

Figure 18

Candlelight	Dangerous to flying birds: burning, death by incineration!

Everyday Dangers

Source of Danger	Consequences
Empty decorative vases	Slipping inside and not being able to get out unaided: suffocation, starvation, heart attack! (Fill the vases with sand or paper.)
Beer mugs, other large containers of liquid	Slipping inside, drowning, suffocation! (Cover them, or empty them and turn them over.)
Knitting work, crocheting work	Getting claws trapped, being hanged!
Yarn, twine, chain	Getting tangled up and strangling!
Hard floors	Birds not fully capable of flying may fall hard upon landing: bone fracture, breast bruises!
Inappropriate spaces between bars in cage or aviary	Head may be stuck through: strangulation or panic and injury!
Wire that is too thin or too sharp	Injuries of toes and head!
Perches that are too thin	Deformity of claws, formation of callus!
Pointed objects, ends of wire, nails, splinters	Injuries, stab wounds!
Human feet	Being trampled underfoot!

Figure 19

Source of Danger	Consequences
Chairs, seats, couches	Being crushed by being sat on!
Poisons	Deadly poisons: lead, copper acetate, rust, synthetically coated pans, any type of detergent, mercury! Also harmful: pencil points, ballpoint pens, felt-tip pens, alcohol, coffee, sharp seasonings!
Insecticides	Anything that exterminates insects or vermin is highly dangerous to the bird! Never spray plants in the bird room. Do not bring sprayed plants into the room.
Poisonous plants	Yew tree, narcissus, primrose.
Nicotine	Smoke-filled air is harmful! Nicotine is deadly!
Mites, vermin	Disinfect cage, toys, and favorite places, but never directly dust or spray the bird: suffocation, poisoning! In the case of parasites, take the bird to the veterinarian.
Human food	Tiny amounts of white bread, dried cakes, or individual grains of salt are frequently provided by owners. These are harmful!
Other house pets	Bird and dog: get along well with each other; leave them together but only under supervision in the beginning. Bird and cat: NO! Bird and rabbit, hamster, or guinea pig: yes, but avoid direct contact. Bird and fish: yes, but cover the aquarium to avoid the danger of drowning.

When the Bird Is Sick

A parakeet that doesn't feel good attracts attention through his listless behavior; he hardly plays with his toys, and he shies away from his human friend or his parakeet mate. He sits apathetically on his branch or perch, with his head turned toward the rear and his beak stuck in his back feathers. He doesn't close his eyes constantly. Instead, he still follows everything that goes on in his vicinity but with a weary look. His feathers are ruffled, and he rests on both legs rather than the customary resting position of one leg. Of course, sitting and sleeping on both legs is, by itself, not necessarily a sign of illness. Parakeets do indeed normally sleep resting on one leg while keeping the other leg tucked into their feathers. There are, however, exceptions. Charlie, for instance, has slept all night on two legs for 7 years; only rarely does he tuck a leg into his feathers.

If the parakeet is sick, there will be other signs of illness. You will notice that he

seldom eats and then only very little. He will repeatedly sit ruffled up in front of the seed bowl and only touch the bowl without taking much from it. If the illness is more serious, he may even squat feebly on the cage floor. A sick parakeet may also stay in his favorite spot, but he won't sit upright. Instead he'll "lie" more on his belly on the branch (Figure 20), with his head lightly inclined down the tail, which will also be drooping downward. If the bird is in pain, at times he will occasionally let his wings droop to the side while he snaps at the air (Figure 21). Often a sick parakeet will breathe harder than usual. If you have a pair, you may notice that the sick bird will be preened more often than usual by the healthy one.

Figure 21 *The parakeet fights strenuously for equilibrium when exhausted from egg laying or tormented by pain. The legs-apart stance and snapping at the air are typical.*

Figure 20 *When the parakeet is sick, he lies down more than he sits on his perch. The feathers are ruffled, and the tail droops.*

If you find your bird in a condition like that described above, it is imperative that

42

When the Bird Is Sick

you examine his droppings. Slimy, viscously flowing, watery stools are always a warning sign. Of course, you should note that an occasional watery stool without the parakeet's appearing sick may actually be an innocuous occurrence. Many parakeets pass watery stools for a short while after bathing, and a great number also react in this manner upon being frightened or when confronted with situations that they do not understand and that cause them discomfort. This can also occur when they are sad, suddenly feel neglected, or are treated badly.

In addition to an impression of general malaise and the possibly altered droppings, mucus can be produced as a visible symptom by the throat and crop. The bird will then retch often and shake his head vigorously to get rid of the mucus. You needn't be concerned, however, when you observe a healthy bird snap open his beak many times in succession as he stretches himself vigorously. It has the same effect for him as yawning. You may also ignore it when he makes noises similar to sneezing. Veterinarians have explained to me that for the healthy parakeet the first reaction is an attempt to compensate for a lack of oxygen, and the second is a substitute for using a handkerchief. On the other hand, if mucus is produced it must always be heeded as a sign of an incipient illness.

Small Bird Dispensary

Every bird owner should be prepared with a small supply of equipment for first aid.

The first aid kit should include the following: tweezers, eye dropper, blunt pair of scissors, tincture of iodine, cotton balls, styptic pencil, charcoal, an antibiotic (recommended by the veterinarian), and a small bandage. Important: Always have an infrared bulb ready in case of illness.

First Aid

Either keep the sick bird by himself in a small separate cage, or leave him in his usual cage with his companion separated from him and sheltered in another room. The room must be warm and quiet and should not be brightly lit. Treat the bird with the infrared lamp. Not only does it give off warmth, but also its rays penetrate under the skin of the patient and stimulate blood circulation and metabolism. The blood vessels expand so that harmful matter can be destroyed more quickly. Defensive cells are activated by the rays. The distance of the rays from the bird should be about 16–20 inches. Test the temperature carefully, as it should not exceed 95°F. Conduct this infrared therapy three times daily for about 20–30 minutes. After the therapy, it is very important that the surrounding temperature not be permitted to drop rapidly. Try to maintain the warmth by means of a light bulb shining on the cage from behind a cloth at a temperature of about 95°F. Often the sick parakeet will show a return to cheerful behavior after the first treatment.

In a disease of the respiratory organs, the parakeet will regurgitate his mucus and

Parakeets

have nasal phlegm, or his breathing will be accompanied by a light rattle. Thus you must provide for sufficient humidity with the infrared rays. Your best bet is to put a dish in the cage that is big enough so that the edge of the dish extends beyond the length of the cage tray. Pour a little hot water into the dish. A light vapor will rise and give off humidity. The cage and the dish should be covered with a cloth so that the vapor is directed to penetrate the interior of the cage and the infrared rays will reach the bird. Be alert, however, when your bird is sick, to the slightest convulsive movements or lameness. *Infrared should not be used under these circumstances.*

These first measures need not be the only treatment during a persistent illness. If after a few hours the bird still seems sick to you, you must bring him to the veterinarian without fail or ask the veterinarian to come to you. Transporting the bird can be safe if he is kept at the same temperature as the room he left. Thus use a heated car! Wrap the cage in a warm blanket (if possible, with an extra, heated electric blanket), or cover it with a heating pad. Note, however, that the bird still needs enough air to breathe.

Advice for handling: If the bird must be taken in your hand for any kind of treatment, hold him properly with the right hand placed in front of the bird's breast. With the left grasp over the head from above. The head will then be between the index and the middle fingers. For an examination the bird can then be taken in the left hand and observed while lying

Figure 22 *To treat carbuncles hold the bird properly: the head lies between the index and the middle finger; the other fingers hold a leg firmly for treatment.*

prone (Figure 22). Never catch the bird in flight; otherwise he can very easily injure his wing or shoulder joint. If the bird cannot be caught in daylight, wait until evening, when it is always easy to achieve this.

Diseases

Diarrhea
Symptoms: Watery or viscous stools, soiled feathers, apathetic behavior.
Possible causes: Catching cold from drafts, rapid change in temperature, drinking water or bath water that's too cold, spoiled or tainted food, gastritis or enteritis, infection or poisoning.
First measures: Wash the soiled feathers with lukewarm water, and dry thoroughly. Isolate; no greens or fruit; animal charcoal on the seed: in stubborn cases roast the seeds lightly; boiled down water or lukewarm camomile or mint tea; constant warmth; infrared rays.
Treatment: If diarrhea last more than 24 hours, bundle the bird up gently and seek the veterinarian.

When the Bird Is Sick

Constipation
Symptoms: The bird obviously strains in passing stools, and in so doing moves his hind quarters back and forth.
Possible causes: Wrong food, poisoning, internal sickness.
First measures: With the eye dropper trickle a drop of castor oil, olive oil, or seed oil sideways on the tongue. Serve fruit, herbs, and, in particular, sprouted seeds.
Treatment: After about 8 hours drip oil on the tongue again. If the constipation doesn't stop, see the veterinarian.

Egg Binding
Symptoms: The female strains as if she is constipated. Her underbelly is rounded, the feathers around the cloaca stick out, and the cere is bright and smooth. If the egg can't be laid, the female becomes weak, her feathers bristle and move noticeably up and down with the tail, she keeps her eyes closed, and finally she can only sit on the cage floor.
Possible causes: General weakness; first egg; the egg has not formed an outer calcium shell.
First measures: Use infrared rays. Provide moist warmth, which will increase humidity.
Treatment: If the egg hasn't been laid within 1 or 2 hours after the warmth treatment, see the veterinarian.

Lameness
Symptoms: Slight dragging of a leg or gradually increasing impediment of movement.
Possible causes: Vitamin deficiency, wrong food, poisoning, injury.
First measures: Vitamin preparation in the drinking water, fresh greens and fruit, warmth *but no infrared.*
Treatment: Call the veterinarian as soon as possible.

Brain Concussion
Symptoms: Sudden total paralysis or unconsciousness.
Possible causes: An unfortunate fall or bump.
First measures: Put the unconscious bird in a soft, dark spot, with his head higher than his body. If the bird is conscious, use warmth *but no infrared.*
Treatment: See the veterinarian immediately.

Cramps
Symptoms: Initially a noticeable general weakness in the legs; later a disturbance of equilibrium, staggering on the ground, and sitting mostly on the belly. Typical head movements. In the worst stages the head is convulsively twisted to the bird's back or stomach.
Possible causes: Vitamin deficiency.
First measures: Rest, warmth, subdued light, *no infrared.*
Treatment: See the veterinarian immediately.

Inflammation of the Crop
Symptoms: Sniffling, sneezing, coughing, head shaking with secretion of mucus, stopped up nostrils, feathers stuck together on the head, difficulty in breathing.
Possible causes: Catching cold ("Diarrhea," page 44), infections.
First measures: Wash the features with lukewarm water, and dry well by dabbing; infrared with warm vapor.
Treatment: See the veterinarian immediately.

Difficulty in Breathing
Symptoms: Debility, trembling, heavy breathing, shrill or whistling breathing sounds, clutching the bars with the beak, and stretching the neck to get more air.
Possible causes: Catching cold ("Diarrhea," page 44), pneumonia, goiter.
First measures: Infrared with warm vapor.
Treatment: See the veterinarian immediately.

Parakeets

Skin Injuries
Symptoms: Bleeding or encrusted wounds.
Possible causes: Injury from sharp objects, fighting with rivals.
First measures: Clean the feathers or legs with boiled down, lukewarm camomile tea. Rest. Minor wounds heal by themselves.
Treatment: Have major wounds treated by the veterinarian.

Lumps under the Skin
Symptoms: Swollen body areas, small boils.
Possible causes: Pads of fat under the skin, hardening of tissue air pockets. Swollen underside of female mostly from laying eggs. Internal causes, not clear.
First measures: None.
Treatment: See the veterinarian.

Blocked Sebaceous Gland
Symptoms: Thickening of the sebaceous gland on the rump.
Possible causes: Blockage of the adipose duct, tumor of the gland.
First Measures: None.
Treatment: See the veterinarian.

Deformed Claws
Symptoms: Frequently getting caught; overgrown claws may wind up in the shape of a spiral.
Possible causes: Perches that are too thin and smooth, too little movement.
First measures: Bring in natural branches of different thicknesses, and place rough stones in the cage. Shorten the toenails. Holding the bird with the left hand, look at the claws against the light. The dark blood vessels at the tip of the claws will be clearly visible. Cut the claws carefully just up to the blood vessels. Should there be bleeding, press a styptic pencil on the toe. Timorous bird owners may have this done by the veterinarian.

Excessively Long Beak
Symptoms: Frequently the upper and lower beaks grow so far upward or downward that intake of food becomes impossible.
Possible causes: Wrong food, too little use of the beak.
First measures: Provide natural perches or limestone.
Treatment: The veterinarian must shorten the beak. In some cases this must be repeated several times.

Parakeet Mange (Fungus of the Beak)
Symptoms: Funguslike brownish growths on the beak, on the cere, in the vicinity of the eyes, and on the legs. It may start as a scarcely visible grayish white layer.
Possible causes: Very small mites.
First measures: None.
Treatment: See the veterinarian, and treat the bird with the prescribed medication.

Attack of Mites
Symptoms: Frequent scratching, nocturnal restlessness.
Possible causes: Red bird mites
First measures: At night cover the cage with a white cloth. The next morning the mites will be visible as red spots. Disinfect everything, and treat with mite spray. In the course of 1 week repeat five times. If the bird is treated with a special mite spray, the head must be carefully covered during the spraying!
Treatment: Have the veterinarian recommend protective measures for the bird.

Fractures
Symptoms: Fractures of the legs and toes are visible; fractures of the thigh or tibia are hardly noticeable, since the latter are in the interior of the body. Wing fractures are also immediately visible.

When the Bird Is Sick

Figure 23   *This is the correct method of putting on a wing bandage if the humerus is broken.*

Possible causes: Fall, striking the ground; getting stuck.
First measures: Place soft padding on the floor of the cage (crumpled tissues, handkerchiefs). Remove all perches. Apply a˙bandage (Figure 23).
Treatment: See the veterinarian immediately.

Normal Molting (not a sickness)
Symptoms: More or less heavy shedding of feathers, up to the point of inability to fly.
Cause: Necessary renewal of feathers.
First measures: Vitamin- and mineral-rich foods, sprouted seeds, greens, fruit, calcium. Increase warmth and rest.
Treatment: In case of very heavy molting, older birds may become very weak and ailing. Use, in addition, infrared rays up to three times a day.

Molting Due to Stress
Symptoms: The bird loses whole tufts of feathers.
Possible causes: Sudden fright, extreme measures against enemies.
First measures: Rest, warmth, vitamin- and mineral-rich foods, sprouted seeds.

French Molt
Symptoms: At the age of 4 weeks young birds lose the pinions and flight feathers, which have already sprouted. They remain flightless and are therefore called runners or jumpers.
Possible causes: Not fully explained; possibly caused by a deficiency of nourishment in the first days of life or by heredity.
First measures: Varied, high-quality food. The most spacious cages possible with fresh branches and limbs for climbing.
Treatment: None; runners remain incapable of flight during most of their lives.

Psittacosis
Symptoms: Apathetic behavior, diarrhea, mucous discharge from the nose. If transmitted to people, the disease makes its appearance in a manner similar to pneumonia and can lead to death, even today, in from 2 to 4 percent of the cases. With children there is the danger of meningitis.
Possible causes: A contagious disease transmitted by bacteria or viruses, first discovered in parrots, now extremely rare. Nonetheless, all parrots must be quarantined. Since the disease can also be transmitted through other kinds of birds, today we use the more general term "orinthosis."
First measures: Isolation, rest, warmth, high-quality food, infrared rays, with warmth and moisture.
Treatment: See the veterinarian immediately.

Putting a Bird to Death

Only the veterinarian should put an animal to death—and then only if its extended life means a danger to others or if the animal itself is suffering. However, as long as an animal is regarded by the law as just "a thing," one can, for a fee, have a

completely healthy bird put to death by
many veterinarians by using an excuse such
as having an allergic reaction to the bird.
This step, therefore, is left to the
conscience of the individual. Nevertheless,
if a bird must be put to death for whatever
reason, this should be done by the
veterinarian.

What to Do with the Bird When . . .

The customary joy of planning for a vacation may be somewhat clouded by the question: What to do with the parakeet?

It would be best for him if he stayed at home in his usual surroundings. If it's a question of a bird pair, one need not worry that the birds will feel lonely and be sad when left alone. A couple can be well tended by a reliable guardian who once a day (preferably in the morning) will provide abundantly for the birds and air the room. This can be someone who lives in your house, a neighbor, or a relative. With a single parakeet the thought of his being alone for a week is troublesome. Ideally, a family member should be at home to give the parakeet some hours of company. If this is not feasible, then one might best bring the little fellow to friends or relatives, who will take care of him. Leave a sufficient supply of the usual seed food, sand, his bathhouse, his toys, and a legibly written small list of instructions, including the special habits of the bird, the fresh supplementary foods he likes best, and the amount of these he should receive daily. Also, indicate whether and how often he bathes. It is crucial to spell out clearly, in detail, the precautions that must be observed in order to avoid accidents. (For a list of dangers see p. 40.)

I'm somewhat skeptical of the frequently heard advice to board the bird in a pet shop during a vacation. Such boarding is feasible only with a parakeet that is accustomed to living by himself and without freedom. A bird that is used to freedom will have the din of voices of the other animals in the pet shop, and perhaps he can even look out at his own species and cultivate voice contact with them, but he will try to escape from the cage the first time the sand tray is removed. It is exceedingly difficult to catch a frightened bird in a store in which the entrance door is constantly being opened. Even if one is successful, it is certainly a panicky experience for all concerned.

If no suitable bird-sitter is found, you can certainly leave the bird alone in the house for 2 or 3 days. In this case, distribute the seed mixture generously in several shallow dishes, because the seeds under the empty shells are no longer accessible to the parakeet. You can also use a dependable food dispenser, provided that it functions reliably and the bird knows how to use it; if this is not the case, your bird will starve! In addition several dishes of millet can be left. Water must be available in the automatic water bottle, but the bird must already be familiar with its use.

I personally find it completely impossible to leave a bird alone in the house for several weeks. Should no other acceptable solution be found, I advise you to advertise for someone to board a parakeet. You can also call the student employment service of your local college and hire a reliable student to care for the bird. Perhaps you could also find some golden ager who might be willing to care for the bird in your home for payment.

As soon as you have brought your parakeet home for the first time, try to arrange a reliable substitute guardian for him. One may not plan to travel but may be required to do so. A person might even be suddenly brought to a hospital. You should guard against these unforeseen events as best you can while still in a position to do so. In extreme cases you can contact an animal protection agency.

Because we must touch on the uncertainties of life here, I would like to ask: What becomes of the parakeet if his human partner dies? You should provide for your parakeet in your will and also indicate where he is to be brought, instead of abandoning him to an uncertain fate.

Parakeet Breeding

Pair Bonding

Observing the gentle, often touching togetherness of a parakeet pair is one of the most beautiful experiences of a bird fancier. If the two also draw their owner into their friendship, their joint happiness is complete. Do not assume, however, that the match will be perfect if one day you simply bring home a mate for a parakeet that lives by himself. First of all, the reciprocal acquaintanceship must be made. First approaches will be shy and hesitant, until the male takes over the role of the father or the protector. The female will take this solicitude for granted, but for a time she will keep her distance and from the beginning will insist on her rights. By nature a male parakeet will never impose his will on the female by force, no matter how gentle she may be. Beyond that the male, vis-à-vis the female, possesses an innate reluctance to aggression, which the female fully relies on. Thus the male will show respect for the female's favorite perching spot. Only when the female stays at a proper distance from it will the male dare to sit there. It will also take a while before the female will permit him to sit near her and then only at an agreeable distance. Perhaps the female will chase him away from his beloved mirror, or maybe she will argue with him about his bell. If the male sits in front of the food bowl, the female may also feel impelled to eat and will choose to eat from his bowl instead of her own.

Birds that live together frequently share moods. If one cleans himself, the other will also begin feather preening; if one takes a rest, the other does the same soon afterward; if one eats or drinks, the other wants to do the same. In the wild many birds can seek food at the same time on the ground. In a cage with only one seed bowl, only one piece of apple, only one drinking bowl, the male may at times lose out. My pair, therefore, has double of everything and as a result is happier.

If the female wishes to be fed by the male, she moves close to him, assumes a slightly cowering pose, and looks at him in a demanding fashion. If the male reacts quickly and properly, the female is gentle; if he is unsuccessful in regurgitating food fast enough, the female will push him away. If the female holds her head out to him for feather preening, the male will fulfill this wish without hesitation. The two must have been together for a while, however, before the female will reciprocate with the male's head feathers.

Display Behavior

Over the course of a month the male will grow more self-confident and at times behave boldly toward the female. As a prelude to sexual arousal he will try at every opportunity to step on the female's tail feathers and to hold on tightly to these feathers with his claws. This type of behavior, however, will be engaged in only if the birds are kept in the open or live in a very spacious cage.

The male will also try to grasp the female's tail feathers with his beak and preen them. The female will almost always pull away with a small cry and will peck at him. This often results in a real tug of war between them. At the same time the male likes to make use of objects in order to impress his female; he will claw at the bell in a frenzied manner or make it whirl around his head by bumping it. He will also spread his wings and make wild flights through the room while screeching loudly. His fiery ardor may make hardly any impression on the female as she calmly withdraws to her spot as if the whole thing had nothing at all to do with her. If the male wants to "flirt" with her again, he nudges the female gently with his beak, while nodding his head eagerly and bobbing up and down several times. He may also rapidly say a few words from his standard speech repertoire.

During mating you can clearly see the male's great excitement in his eyes. The pupils narrow to very small, black points, and the white iris is more prominent than ever before. The parakeet's eyes dilate and contract not only when flirting with his female, but also when he mates with a substitute object. He will also ruffle his head feathers at such a time.

Mating and Egg Laying

During these flirtations the pair need not necessarily complete the mating. A pair kept by themselves will miss the stimulation provided by companions that are also in heat. If the play goes further, the male parakeet will copulate with the female many times during the day. Before long the female will finally be ready for mating and will offer herself to the male in an enticing manner.

She will cling firmly to a branch with both feet, stick her somewhat sideways-turned tail high in the air, and lay her head far back. She will remain motionless in this graceful position and stare steadfastly at the male. The latter, in the heat of excitement, will place one foot on the back of the female. He will then bill and coo with her rapidly before he puts both feet on her back while holding himself fast with his beak attached to her head or neck feathers (Figure 24).

Figure 24 *Mating by parakeets lasts only for seconds. When the cloacas of both birds touch, the female's tail is raised.*

The male then places both wings forward and thus embraces the female and brings his cloaca into contact with hers. I have seen this type of mating behavior with my

52

pair of parakeets. I have also read descriptions of variations in which, during the mating procedure, the couple intertwine their beaks, or the male through the vigorous shaking of his buttocks touches the female's cloaca on an alternating basis. Other descriptions indicate that the female lets her wings hang. I've never seen that.

When the mating is over, both birds shake their feathers and the female leaves the area. The male follows her and starts to feed her. If a nesting box is present, the female will take refuge in it and the male will feed her through the sliding hole. If the mating urge of the female continues, she may offer herself many times daily during the egg-laying period. During this time the male will constantly wait with the female, but he is not yet ready to mount her. The act is finally consummated, however, in a few seconds through the shaking of the feathers.

Before a young female lays her first egg, you probably will be somewhat nervous because many females appear slightly ill 1 or 2 days before egg laying. They often make their bodies narrow and fold their wings, while slightly trembling. If you watch the female closely, you will notice that her cere has gotten brighter and smoother than before. In addition, the female often gnaws noticeably on the limestone for days in advance. Eventually you find the first egg on the cage floor. Without a nest box the female's egg may not be noticed at all; often it can be destroyed or eaten along with the shell.

After laying her eggs the female will use all of her strength to once again claw her way up to a perch. On this high point it is an effort to keep her balance. She is thin and tense as she spreads her trembling wings and bites the empty air. If the male is still present, he will seek a rough and tumble contact with the female, which at this time can barely summon enough strength to hold onto the perch. This faulty estimate of the situation by the male can be explained only by the unnatural egg laying. In nature the egg is laid in the nesting hole, the male is not present, and the female does not have to strain to balance herself on a perch after the effort. She then lies on her belly in the nesting place and can relax more easily.

Once a laying period has begun, the female lays four to six (occasionally seven or eight) eggs even if no nest box is at her disposal.

Many females look for a hiding place for their eggs. They slip into a box; they lay their eggs in the corner or in a bookcase, behind books. Or they may simply let the eggs fall on the floor of the cage. A female tries only rarely to breed without a nest box.

Incubation

If you want parakeet offspring you must provide the pair with a nest box (Figure 25). This can be purchased for just a few dollars in a 10 × 6 × 6 inch size. On one side of the wall is the entrance hole with a small perch underneath it. On the opposite side, on the floor of the next box, is the flat nesting dish. You should be able to

Parakeets

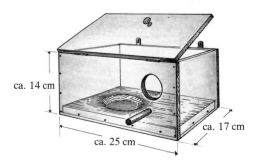

ca. 14 cm

ca. 25 cm

ca. 17 cm

Figure 25 *There are nest boxes for sale in pet shops. Make sure that the nesting dish and the entrance hole are not arranged one above the other.*

open the cover of the box so you can view the inside.

Before you buy a nest box, give the matter some serious thought. If your pair is young and healthy and has mated repeatedly, you can look forward to five or six young parakeets. But you then have a responsibility to the young ones, just as the parents do. Do you wish to keep all the birds? There are questions of space, future breeding, quadrupled increase in work due to nursing, and increased costs. All these points must be considered beforehand. If you don't wish to keep the fledglings, decide whether you have enough friends to take the parakeets from your brood. If you are certain of being able to surmount these problems, then hang the nesting box in the cage in a protected place in the room. Do not place it so high that you cannot watch the additional action.

At first both parakeets will avoid the unfamiliar box, just as they will anything else that's new. But after a few hours, when the female has taken the breeding box for granted, she will start to inspect it. Soon she will probably be sitting in the nest box and chewing on the entrance hole and on the walls. Now the male no longer has to court his mate. The eggs will follow the mating on a schedule of one every 2 days. The female will incubate these eggs day and night for 4 weeks. The male will stay for hours on the perch in front of the entrance hole. Now and then he will poke his head inside and feed the female through the hole. If the female wants to rest, however, and the male ventures too far inside with his head, the shriek of the female will resound. Even you should now avoid opening the cover and disturbing her. Be careful not to put your finger within range of the female, or she'll bite it with all her might in defense of her brood.

Among the fertilized eggs there can also be unfertilized ones. You must examine the eggs in the absence of the female. You will recognize the unfertilized ones after about 10 days of incubation when you hold them up to the light. They will be clear and transparent. Fertilized eggs, on the other hand, have a light bluish gleam and appear darker. If the female has laid only a few eggs, leave the unfertilized eggs beside the fertilized ones. In this way the newly hatched youngsters will later have a soft support to protect them from their mother's weight.

The manner in which the breeding and rearing of the young proceeds is described in the chapter about the life of the Australian parakeets (page 59). During the

Parakeet Breeding

coming weeks, which are strenuous for the birds, they need food that is especially rich in variety. The bird room must be constantly maintained at the same temperature. It must have fresh air and some humidity (hang a vaporizer over the radiator, or use a humidifier).

During the first 4 weeks the male has only a few duties. To some extent he will feed the female, but she also feeds herself to a large degree. At this time (with the female emerging from the next box for only a few minutes) the male will feel somewhat lonesome and will gladly seek the company of his owner. Give him a lot of attention during these weeks, and above all try not to change anything in the vicinity of the breeding box because the female reacts to these things in a very sensitive manner.

Hatching and Rearing

Even before the babies hatch, you should furnish the parents with special breeding food which contains vital nutrients. If the parents get used to it early, the babies will receive first-rate nourishment. The first soft peeping should resound from the box after 21 days.

If everything has proceeded smoothly up to this point, you can now fully entrust the beginning of the babies' training to the parents. Despite your enormous curiosity do not disturb the female too often by opening the cover. Check on the youngsters once a day, but it's best to do so when the female has left the area. The young parakeets will lie like balls in the nest with their hard little heads on the floor (Plate 6). The smallest naked one will for the most part be covered by the older siblings. If the number of siblings is too great, the last born can be crushed to death. If you should find a dead baby in the nest, remove it right away.

From the 10th day of life on, the first down feathers will begin sprouting on the tiny nestlings. After 15 days the large feathers will become visible. With a young parakeet the plumage is developed to such an extent by 18 days that you can take him out of the nest and examine him carefully. Be careful how you put the little borrowed creature back in the nest as long as the mother is sheltering her other offspring under her wing. You may not under any circumstances simply thrust the baby back through the entrance hole, because the protective mother will furiously strike with her beak at anything penetrating from the outside, as if it were an enemy, and could in her great rage kill her own child.

From the 26th day on, the young parakeet possesses his own full set of feathers; soon afterward he will also leave the nest. You must see to it beforehand that after leaving the nest the babies find appropriate shelter. They will need an ideal location because the youngsters will be strengthening their wings all day long while they fasten themselves to a branch or perch and flap their wings powerfully back and forth. The first flights, on the other hand, are made dangerous by their unnatural environment. The little ones are capable of flying, but they cannot "brake" in time and thus they fly into the aviary wall, bump against it, and fall fluttering to the ground.

Parakeets

Fortunately the speed of their flight is not so great that they can seriously hurt themselves.

An aviary furnished with many branches considerably helps the youngsters' awkward landings and their initial difficulties with flying. The young birds also stand a greater chance of success if they can fly to the wire mesh and land there. If the fledglings must take their first flights within a room, then during the first weeks you should stretch several heavy-duty ropes at different heights. These have the right diameter and are soft so that the birds can hold fast to them. In addition, branches and perches brought in from the outside will also help. The ideal would be a bird room with sand spread on the floor. There the youngsters could live together and also seek food. They could also undertake short flights from the perch to the rope and thus improve their skills.

Understanding Parakeets: A Special Chapter

A Tiny Australian Animal

Everyone who lives with parakeets often asks him- or herself why these birds do this, but not that, and why many aspects of their behavior are so very different from those of European birds.

If one reads accounts of the life of the parakeets in Australia, he or she can understand in a much better fashion why the birds have developed precisely these typical behavior patterns for their species.

Parakeet Life in the Treeless Plains and Semiwilderness

Originally all Australian parrots and parakeets were probably forest inhabitants. By the end of the Pleistocene age, the older period of the geological new era, large parts of the Australian continent had begun to dry out. For the parrots and parakeets a need arose to adapt themselves to the new ecological conditions in the dry regions. The parakeets succeeded especially well. The small parakeet, at one time an inhabitant of the Australian tropical forest (as it still is, even today, in the northern part of the continent), not only adapted to life on the bush prairie, but even held its own in the semiwilderness, which abounded only in prickly porcupine grass.

Today the "betcherrygah" (so called by the original inhabitants of Australia) is spread over almost the entire continent. It prefers open country and avoids the dense forest regions, as well as the land strips close to the coast. It prefers to stay on the shores of creeks; these are brooks or river courses that only periodically carry water. High eucalpytus trees grow there, and they become the actual "trees of life" for the parakeets (Plate 8).

The bird can exist in an environment that is markedly hostile to life. The temperatures in the dry regions hover on the average between 86 and 95°F, but at times can climb to 113°F in the shade. At night, below-freezing temperatures can prevail for hours. Rainfalls occur irregularly. In the south of the continent frequent rain is expected in the winter months. In the north it rains more in the summer months, but one still cannot speak of steady rain periods. During the days the smaller plants wither, the water dries up, and only large trees (mainly eucalyptus trees, grass trees, acacias, and spinifex) retain their foliage and provide the parakeet with shade and camouflage. During these periods the birds can find food only in dried grain seeds, which are lacking in protein and devoid of moisture.

Observers of wild parakeets have spoken of the "secretive way of life" of these birds. It is understandable how this would stem from the extreme environmental conditions under which the parakeets live in groups of 10–50 birds. During the day, especially in the hours of intense heat, they sit quietly in the tree branches. Thanks to their green camouflage they avoid the eyes of their enemies. The yellow spots on their feathers have the same effect as the play of sunlight on the green foliage. Many trees, because of hordes of birds sitting in them, appear to be covered with yellow flowers (Plate 8). The peculiarly effective motionlessness of

Parakeets

the birds is nothing more than an essential compensation for the lack of moisture. Movement increases the need for oxygen in a living creature. Lung activity increases, whereby body moisture evaporates to a greater degree. Thus the parakeet is forced to "conserve" because of lack of moisture. The parakeet is able to increase this "dry adjustment" for an emergency to such an extent (as was demonstrated in an experiment) that it can survive in humidity of only 30 percent and in a mean temperature of 80°F for 3 weeks without taking a drop of water.

In the cooler morning and afternoon hours the parakeets wander about in groups, in search of food, deep into the country. In the hot hours of the day they retreat back to the sheltering tree foliage. In the morning and evening they regularly visit the closest water spots. In times of extreme drought the parakeet groups cluster together in hordes of thousands of birds and roam the countryside in search of food. In this way during the last few decades the Australian parakeets have made use of human artifacts by drinking out of reservoirs and artificially constructed watering places designed for livestock. Australian farmers have reported hordes of parakeets that joined thousands, even millions, of other birds in this practice. These artificial reservoirs, with vertical concrete walls, can sometimes become deathtraps for thousands of birds. The thirsty animals push to reach the water with such force that the birds already drinking are pushed into the water by the late arrivals. As many as 30,000 drowning birds were saved from one artificial pond. One

farmer had to shovel 5 tons of bird carcasses from his livestock trough. Despite these gigantic losses the parakeet population multiplies in rainy periods with uncommon rapidity.

Mating and Incubation Take Place When It Rains

A striking example of the parakeet's outstanding powers of adaptability is the speed with which it compensates for the annually recurring loss of thousands. The mating seasons of the songbirds with which we are familiar are dependent on the length of the days (a result of the position of the sun), but the parakeet knows no fixed mating season. All the internal hormonal processes that are prerequisites for the birds to mate and hatch eggs occur in the parakeet when it starts to rain or when, during its extensive travels, it reaches areas that have just had heavy rainfalls. The bird will then be active and filled with energy from dawn to dusk, and it will also be ready for pairing and mating. The female wiil seek a nesting place and thus fall into the mating mood.

The mature parakeet can subsist for months on end on dried seeds and with a minimum of moisture, but for the rearing of the young semiripe seeds are essential. After the rain the plants begin to grow and develop. During this time the females lay their eggs and hatch them. When the first babies emerge, the parents already have found the food necessary for the rearing of the brood. As long as the moisture and the growth of the green plants continue, the crowd of birds will stay in the fertile area and will start a second brood right after the first, and may even begin a third. Then, if an oncoming drought compels the parakeets to resume their nomadic life, even the last-born baby birds will be fledged and capable of joining the flock.

The female parakeet does not have to take time to build a nest. For nesting she uses available natural crevices situated in openings in the highest branches of the eucalyptus trees. The available decayed matter at the bottom of the hole is most satisfactory as padding for the eggs. As the female vigorously enlarges the hole or its entrance, tiny chips fall in which also serve as extra padding. Even when several trees are available for nesting in a flock's breeding area, all the couples of one group nest together in one tree. Obviously, this social breeding is a sign of adaptation because the short time available for the preservation of the species must be used to the utmost by all the pairs. The ritual of mating and the activity of nesting, taking place immediately afterward, encourage couples that were not yet in the right frame of mind to proceed with their own mating and breeding. In the space of 2 days the female will lay five to eight eggs in the nesting hole and hatch them by herself. The male stays close to the hole, but it is not clear whether he is keeping watch or remaining there because the parakeet is accustomed to living as part of a group. During the incubation he feeds the female through the entrance to the nest. He is allowed into the nesting hole only when the

babies have already grown larger and are fed jointly by him. Not every female allows the father to come into the nest. Often the male must wait to participate in feeding the babies until they can fly out of the nest.

Parakeets have an active metabolism, and they excrete often. The white, nonliquid urine portion is surrounded by a dark ring of solid droppings. From observing my parakeets I know that such droppings appear every 15–20 minutes. They are odorless and leave no stains. Since an incubating female does not dare deposit her feces directly in the nest for fear of attracting enemies, she must leave the nest for this purpose. Of course, leaving every 15 or 20 minutes would harm the brood. Therefore the metabolism of the female is already significantly regulated before depositing the first egg, so that she has to leave the nest only every 2–3 hours. In addition, after laying the last egg, the female starts a light molt. Many authors are of the opinion that the female tears out her feathers as an extra source of warmth for her babies, but I have never been able to observe this practice. I believe that the molting process has two advantages. First, the feathers falling from the female into the nest actually keep the babies warm. Second, both parents use this time of reduced flight activity to partly replenish their coats.

Growing Up in Three Months

After an incubation period of 18 days the babies pass through successive stages of

Plate 7 *This outstanding photo by Australian* ▷
animal photographer Norman Chaffer shows a
wild male parakeet feeding a baby bird at the
entrance to the nesting hole.

development. The female feeds the still very small nestlings with a secretion from her crop produced especially for her brood. After a few days the chicks that are maturing receive the predigested food from the crop, while the smaller ones are fed from the maw. In order to guarantee these differentiations in feeding, the baby birds that were hatched first are always fed first. After emptying her crop for the older chicks, the mother regurgitates the contents of the maw to feed the younger ones.

When there are babies in the nest, the female will leave infrequently to deposit droppings, to eat quickly, and to clean herself. The female receives most of the necessary food from the male, and it is likewise predigested in the crop. In this way there is a constantly ready supply of predigested food at the disposal of the little ones. If the female had to prepare the food herself in her crop, valuable time would be lost. The breeding operation is always working against the clock because it is always uncertain how long the favorable feeding conditions will last. Thus everything is geared so that the parakeet brood will grow rapidly and become fully fledged.

For 2 or 3 weeks the female shelters her young. Their grayish white down drops off at the time that the first coat of feathers appears. The rearing progresses according to plan and in a highly rational manner. No time is wasted even in removing the droppings of the babies from the nest, and evidently this does no harm. In many reports there are allusions to tiny parasites that feed in the nest on the babies' droppings. The young leave the nest after about 4 weeks. By then they are able to fly and are self-reliant. However, they are still cared for by the father for 1 or 2 more weeks and are even occasionally fed by him. During this time the female (often even before the last of the young birds has become fledged) has already started with the second hatching if food conditions permit.

During the first 3 months the newly fledged parakeet wears his youthful coat of feathers, which doesn't differ essentially from that of the older bird. The feathers already have the typical designs, but the colors are noticeably duller. The yellow facial mask is only hinted at, and the wavy design or striations on the back of the head extend above the top of the head and forehead down to the cere. The cere itself is bright and gives only a hint of the bird's sex. Most impressive are the big, black shoe-button eyes of the young parakeets. The visible eye consists only of the pupil. The white iris in the fully grown parakeet becomes clearly visible only in exceptional cases (for example, in flirtation). It is first formed at the same time as the coat of feathers of the sexually mature parakeet and makes the pupil seem smaller. After 3 months the young bird begins molting. Thereafter he is the equal of the older birds and is also sexually mature. Should the flock again find a suitable breeding area, even the youngest generation can contribute to the preservation of the species. (With the domesticated parakeet the youthful molting for birds hatched in the spring begins after 3 months; for autumn "chicks" it begins the following spring.)

] Plate 8 *A swarm of parakeets in the Australian wilderness. The need for companionship and contact with their own species is still markedly strong even in tame parakeets.*

The Parakeet's Enemies

In their quest for food and water the birds continue to roam in groups or flocks covering long stretches and descending to fertile areas as long as food supplies last. They again make use of the cooler morning and evening hours to look for food on the ground. Semiripe grass and vegetable seeds are preferred, but in time of need they content themselves with dried grain. Thus, with the aid of their prehensile beaks and clambering feet, they skillfully climb up the higher shrubs and brushwood. The birds also ingest coarse sand with their food as an aid to digestion. It is not clear whether small insects are part of the nourishment typical of this species or whether they are swallowed by mistake.

While the birds are seeking food on the ground and eating, drinking, or even bathing in the dew-moistened grass, they stay perfectly still. This makes sense, as in this situation the parakeets are defenseless against their archfoes, the condors. Should a falcon or other bird of prey invade such a parakeet group, he can seize at least one victim. Most of the time it is a sick or older bird that was not fast enough to escape. The others fly shrieking and screaming to the next tree, where they are protected against enemies of this kind.

The greatest foe of the Australian parakeets is the long dry periods, in which (depending on the area) not a drop of rain may fall for 12 months or more. During these periods hundreds of thousands of parakeets die from lack of food and water. Other enemies of the parakeet are snakes and savage European house cats which human beings have brought to Australia. In the house cat the parakeet has a ground foe against which no inborn hostile behavior can protect him.

Parakeets fly fast and persistently. Their flying altitude for the most part surpasses the height of the highest trees. If the birds fly in great swarms, their flight appears purposeful and comparable to that of a host of starlings. In this compact crowd they are greatly protected against birds of prey. Single birds and smaller groups fly more slowly and in bow-shaped or wave line patterns. When in danger, parakeets first remain motionless so that at the last moment they can fly off with a shriek and, with the speed of an arrow, find the next tree. When the danger appears to be over, they fly back to the group's tree.

Life in the Flock

In spite of what we know of the parakeet's wild life on its home ground, very few details about its behavior are available to us. Nevertheless, we can be sure that the parakeet, as a member of the family of parrots, belongs to the most highly developed group of birds. This group has impressed human beings by its above average intelligence and manifold examples of innate and acquired behavior. The members of a parakeet group, especially the mating pairs, know each other personally. The unions last for life, and only the death of a partner can be the occasion for a new pair formation. The

Parakeets

cohesiveness of the group and of the individual couples is strengthened by reciprocal preening of feathers. The males feed their females even after the mating season to solidify the union, birds superior in rank feed birds inferior in rank, probably to ensure the cohesiveness of the group and the hierarchy.

Flight and Landing Maneuvers

Parakeets are by nature nimble flyers. They quickly learn to know the available space at their disposal, and they use it skillfully in terms of longitude and latitude for their flight. The birds like to use several landing places; these are regarded as a parakeet's private property and respected as such by his partner. Parakeets are able to perceive quite well from the noise of the flight whether a bird is flying to change from one place to another, whether he wants to impress his partner by flying, or whether he's inviting the other one to fly with him. A flight to change places is performed without haste or sound. In a flight to make an impression the male executes great circles and lands on the spot from which he took off. In an invitation to fly with him the inviter emits a loud shriek and flies away over the partner or close by the other bird. This invitation is fruitless if the female is sick or feels obligated to remain in the nesting box. A bird may often leave its place quite without reason, with a loud cry, in "a flight of fear." In so doing he unhesitatingly drags his partner with him. This lightning-quick rushing away differs significantly from other flights. The flight of

fear is accompanied by a loud warning cry. Afterwards the bird often does not have sufficient time to find a familiar landing place. This can easily result in a hasty, forced landing on an object hitherto avoided. Obviously the parakeet also has an urge to fly up and away every once in a while with a loud warning cry, for no known reason.

Expression of Moods

From time to time the bird, when in a threatening or dangerous situation, will utter a warning cry or shriek of fear in what I have called an "expression of mood." Before falling asleep the sound of gentle beak sharpening can be heard, and during peaceful inactivity one can often detect a songlike twittering. Quiet feeding may be accompanied by deep cooing, and an amorous approach by clear, rythmically clicking sounds. The intensely loud, scolding cries of parakeets may generally be interpreted as the release of excess energy, although they sound like anger or indignation. To express repressed, joyful, or erotic emotions the parakeet rumbles gently and almost melodiously.

Hearing, Seeing, Smelling, Curiosity, and Fear

A parakeet can hear as well as a human being. He accepts familiar noises without any special reaction. He responds to loud explosions and unusual noises, according to their intensity, with either a warning cry, a

Understanding Parakeets: A Special Chapter

frightened flight, or careful listening while maintaining a pose that makes his body look narrow.

Parakeets can see just as well as human beings. It has even been said that birds are the "eyes of man." Everything new and unusual is viewed suspiciously, and even the smallest details are noticed by the parakeet. Either he peers cautiously at the unknown object with a tilted head, or, if need be, he slides backward or sideways and makes his body narrow, or he takes to flight in a terrified manner. On the other hand, the parakeet is curious. He investigates everything thoroughly but always with a mixture of apprehension and curiosity.

The parakeet is sensitive to very bright light. Many birds become frightened if a bright light is turned on suddenly at twilight. You can spare your bird this fright if you first cover the light bulb with your hand and let the gleam appear gradually. The bird will feel out of sorts if he is bombarded directly by lamplight.

How well can a parakeet smell? I'm not able to say. One expert is of the opinion that the parakeet's sense of smell is just as good as that of a human being.

Sex Objects

The sexual behavior of the parakeet has already been described in detail (page 51). Males kept by themselves may copulate with a surrogate object instead of with a female. This can be a small plastic replica of a parakeet, a ball, a bell, a wristwatch, or the ear lobe or nose of his human friend. Frequently, one sees a male bowing before a branch or simply bowing passionately into the empty air, gently twittering and pattering along with contracted pupils. Meanwhile his mirror is fed, or the nose of his owner is stuffed with pulp. If this displeases you, you should pair your parakeet with a female early on. If the bird becomes accustomed to satisfying his drives with a surrogate object, it may well be that he will no longer act true to type toward a female if one becomes available.

Routines

Parakeets are routine conscious. They feel well and safe when certain events always occur in the same manner. Going to bed, for example, should be prefaced nightly with the same unvarying words, which should be repeated right up to the time the light is put out. When I come home, Charlie insists on a ceremonial greeting, which is always given in the same way. Even with bathing there are firm "rules." Such routines will occasionally be varied, but it takes a long time for them to be abandoned and replaced by new ones.

Are Parakeets Intelligent?

I consider parakeets to be quite intelligent. For an animal with a body weight of only a few ounces they are, in my eyes, amazingly clever.

A completely objective report from the behavioral scientist Otto Koenig dealt with the ability of various animals to count after training. The parakeet, as well as the

Parakeets

jackdaw, was successful, through picking up seeds, in reaching the number 6. The dove reached the number 5; the common raven, the number 7.

The speech of the parakeet is due to the bird's pleasure in mimicry. It has nothing to do with the ability to think, but it is obvious that isolated words or sentences are connected with definite situations and applied logically. For example, Charlie always says, "Excuse me, please; I have to clean my nose," whenever he sees me bring a handkerchief to my nose. When listening to "his" tape recorder, with which he is very familiar, he fills in the pauses with the words that are to follow.

The recognition of certain objects is not surprising in a parakeet with good eyesight. He distinguishes precisely between objects that are similar in appearance and accurately picks out the familiar and preferred one. Charlie prefers to play with balls that consist of round latticework and have a little bell rolling inside them. I keep about 20 of these little balls on hand in order always to have a replacement. He is used to a particular one, however, and plays exclusively with it. If I exchange the ball, he rejects the new one after the first touch and mournfully looks for the right one. If I give the right one back with three wrong ones, he runs happily to the favorite and separates it. The wrong ones go unnoticed.

Parakeets have a marked sense of order. Their bowls, their greens, and everything else that they are familiar with must constantly be found in their proper place, or momentary confusion will occur.

Parakeet Problems

Tame parakeets will fly away from their trusted owners when they are extremely frightened. In the case of minor fears they retreat into other forms of behavior. One expert noted that, when a bird's curiosity and uncertainty get the better of him, he is faced with a dilemma. I have noted this in my observations of Charlie. He likes to play with me and push small spinning balls off the table with his beak. He is, however, uncomfortable when one or two of the balls approach him from the side instead of the front. His reaction is to immediately run to his dish on my writing desk and start to eat. If I remove some of the balls, the situation again becomes manageable for him and he resumes the game.

Although all parakeets speak with a characteristic "speech," not one resembles another in nature and temperament. An owner who wants to fully understand his or her parakeet should not only correctly interpret the basic patterns of behavior that are common to all these birds, but also, through an intensive relationship with the parakeet, learn the types of behavior that are peculiar to this particular one.

Body Language and Speech

You can see quite clearly when a parakeet is frightened, feels generally good, or looks at something with curiosity or skepticism. As small as he is, the bird has at his disposal a wide range of expressions. He can use his changeable voice and his

Understanding Parakeets: A Special Chapter

acrobatically gifted body to make himself well understood to his own species and to the human observer.

What Does It Mean When the Parakeet . . .

Scratching the head: When a parakeet chooses to scratch his head, he doesn't simply bring a leg upward; rather, he first pushes it through and under his feathers and then brings it up to his head (Figure 26).

Figure 27 *When the parakeet stretches his leg to the rear, it is a sign of well-being and is comparable to our lolling about.*

Figure 26 *If the parakeet wants to scratch his head, he brings his leg under his wing and then to his head.*

Scratching toward the rear: From time to time the parakeet will scratch both legs, one after the other, far to the rear (Figure 27). In drawing them back, the bird generally clenches the toes into a little fist. Often the fist is missing, but there is always a stretching of the legs. If you notice that your parakeet constantly stretches only one leg (and always the same one), or does not engage in this necessary movement, you should suspect that this may be the beginning of a pathological weakness (stemming from a vitamin deficiency, p. 45).

Sitting on one leg: The stretching of the legs frequently ends with one leg being drawn into the feathers. Sitting on only one leg indicates calmness as the bird babbles or twitters softly to himself.

Sticking the head into the feathers: The parakeet can turn his head 90° to the rear in a lofty feeling of well being as he buries his beak into his feathers (Figure 28). If the babbling stops gradually, it is a sign that the bird has fallen asleep. Many birds fall asleep while sitting on both legs. Many birds can also sit upright on both legs. You also often hear the soft sounds which the bird produces by lateral beak sharpening. These also show a feeling of well-being.

Feather care: The bird's supple agility can be observed when he cleans himself. This is done daily, on and off over a period of

Parakeets

Figure 28 *Sleeping position of the parakeet: the head is turned to the rear and buried in the back feathers.*

hours, in order to take care of all the many individual feathers involved. The parakeet pulls them skillfully through his beak (Plate 2) and thereby smooths them and removes their dirt. He reaches every place on his body with astonishing stretches of his beak; the head is reached with the feet. The bird skillfully uses his beak to bring oil from the sebaceous gland on the upper side of its rump. The oil is then spread over the feathers. This light, oily film serves as a protection against moisture as well as for feather care. The parakeet will often brush his head on a perch or on a corner of the cage in order to scratch himself quickly and vigorously. After molting thére is a crucial need for new feathers to grow. These are first hidden in a delicate sheath and unfold only when this cover bursts and falls off. After molting, the sheaths fall to the ground like very fine scales. You can recognize the future feathers when they first appear as small round spikes among the old feathers still present.

Cleaning the tail: The parakeet seems to consider his tail his most valuable structure; simply as a matter of self-indulgence, he preens it most frequently (Plate 2). His partner is never allowed to undertake this, and even a hesitant attempt meets with resistance and a cry of anguish. Apparently the parakeet uses his tail (in particular, the tip) as a special sensor that yields information such as the following: contact with thing, unavoidable; or contact with another living object, resist unconditionally!

Raising the wings: The folded wings are raised upward just as frequently as the legs are stretched (Figure 29). This is done for relaxation as well as to get rid of body heat during warm weather. It can also be a sign of great contentment.

Figure 29 *When the parakeet lifts his wings he wants to relax or get rid of excessive body heat.*

Shaking the feathers: Shaking the feathers always follows relief from physical or emotional tension.

Understanding Parakeets: A Special Chapter

Moving the wings sideways: If the parakeet moves his folded wings sideways against himself, or in a rectangular fashion, he is excited.

Biting into the air: If the bird narrows his body and bites into the empty air, he is ill, is in pain, or is experiencing fearful anxiety (Figure 21).

Flexing the wings angularly: If the parakeet flexes his wings "angularly" without narrowing his body, he is attempting to impress a female or a rival, with a certain amount of anxiety involved.

Stepping on another's breast: In a battle between rivals the two males attack each other with ruffled feathers and step on each other's breasts until the struggle gets to be too much for one of them and he darts away like an arrow.

Biting another's feet: Two females fight differently; first of all, they try to bite each other's feet. If one of them is successful, there is an unmistakable shriek of pain from the losing female, who, despite her screaming, is often bitten bloodily.

Biting the owner: Parakeets can take a painful bite with their powerful beaks, either from fear or when they are aggressive. If you must handle a frightened or excited parakeet for some pressing reason, my advice is to put a thin wooden rod in his beak. He will bite on it with all his might without nipping you. Under other circumstances parakeets do not as a rule bite their own species or their owners except out of exuberant playfulness or wild love. The female is not serious in her attempts to bite her partner, even though she may snap at him with her beak. If a battle actually resulted in injuries or even a serious fight, with the male the loser, it would be the basis for a strong aversion to each other.

Defecating: A parakeet should defecate every 15–20 minutes. If he's just sitting on a perch, or on your finger or shoulder, he simply lets nature take its course. If he is sitting on the floor or table, he will remain motionless for a few seconds after the movement. If the bird is easily excited, he will move his bowels more often than normally.

A Request to the Reader

If you have observed parakeet behavior patterns involving speech, body language, or feats of intellect that have not been described in this book, please write to me about them. These should be actions that have been continually repeated by your bird over a long period of time.

Books to Enhance Your Knowledge and Understanding of Parakeets

1. *Enjoy Your Parakeets-Budgies*
   Earl Schneider, Ed.: The Pet Library Ltd.
2. *Best in Show: Breeding and Exhibiting Budgerigars*
   Gerald Binks: Michael Joseph (Merrimac Book Service).
3. *Parakeet Guide*
   Cyril H. Rogers: Doubleday.
4. *How to Live with a Parakeet*
   B. A. Benson: Cornerstone Library
5. *The Budgerigar or Shell Parakeet as a Talker*
   Cessa Feyerabend: American Budgerigar Association

Index

Parakeets